IF LOVE Is
a GAME,
THESE Are
the RULES

CHERIE CARTER-SCOTT, PH,.D.

IF LOVE Is a GAME, THESE Are the RULES

Ten Rules for Finding Love
and Creating Long-Lasting,
Authentic Relationships

Broadway Books New York

BROADWAY

Broadway Books titles may be purchased for business or promotional use or for special sales. For information, please write to: Special Markets Department, Random House, Inc., 1540 Broadway, New York, NY 10036.

BROADWAY BOOKS and its logo, a letter B bisected on the diagonal, are trademarks of Broadway Books, a division of Random House, Inc.

Visit our website at www.broadwaybooks.com

Library of Congress Cataloging-in-Publication Data
Carter-Scott, Chérie.
    If love is a game, these are the rules : ten rules for finding love and creating long-lasting, authentic relationships / by Chérie Carter-Scott.
        p.   cm.
    ISBN 0-7679-0424-9 (hardcover)
    1. Man–woman relationships.   2. Love (Psychology).   I. Title.
    HQ801.C296   1999   99-29795
    306.7—dc21   CIP

FIRST EDITION

Designed by Songhee Kim

99   00   01   02   03   10   9   8   7   6   5   4   3   2

I dedicate this book to Louis Untermeyer, my uncle, who read me his poems of love as I sat at his feet. He was the first person to teach me about writing and love in the same sentence.

I also dedicate this book to Michael, my soul mate, husband, and beloved, who has chosen to be authentic with me and hold my hand in the adventure of life. Without the experience of loving and being loved by him, I would never have written this book.

Acknowledgments

Debra Goldstein, my alter ego, has dedicated her efforts to ensure structure, continuity, integrity, and flow.

Lauren Marino, my editor, who believed in this book and in me, provided guidance, direction, and feedback.

Lynn Stewart, my sister and business partner for 25 years, has been there each step of the way, providing recollections of participants and workshops past, case studies from hundreds of couples, feedback on the text, and her experiences as a couples facilitator. Her support is endless and undaunted.

Leah Nichols, who devoted untold hours and energy editing and proofreading.

Bill Shinker believed in me, in my vision and experience, and in the wisdom of the Game-Rule books.

Bob Barnett and Jackie Davies are my guardian angels to whom I am dearly grateful.

Bill Milham and Sister Christine Bowman, my dear friends, painstakingly proofread this text so it could be the best. Your suggestions were much appreciated.

Judy Rossiter has supported the process and me by "holding" and enrolling the workshops so that I could write this book.

Michael Pomije has been and continues to be my beloved, my soul mate, and my partner in the "Lifeshop" that provides one working model of the authentic relationship.

A special thank you goes to Steven Krasner for all his love and support.

Thanks to all those couples who have trusted me to facilitate them in knowing their stories, issues, secrets, the dynamics and inner workings of their relationships. It is from these experiences that I have been guided in what this book should communicate.

To all those men and women who have taught me what it means to be authentic, thank you for teaching me about relating and relationships. I thank you for your patience and input over the years. I have been a good student and have learned what I could so that I can pass it on to others.

Contents

Rule One

YOU MUST LOVE YOURSELF FIRST

*Your relationship with yourself is the central template
from which all others are formed. Loving yourself is a prerequisite to creating
a successful and authentic union with another.*

1

This book expresses my sentiments and the purpose of my life's work. In my heart, I deeply want couples to understand each other and to be able to authentically express their love. I've devoted my workshops, seminars, and several books to this subject.

With changing roles and soaring divorce rates, men and women today need more help than ever before in finding and keeping love in their lives. At best, we learn from the relationships around us, many of which are less than the ideal role models. We make mistakes and start over again, always asking: What do I need to do in order to build a truly fulfilling and enriching relationship?

Even though we spend our whole lives trying to make relationships work, no one has ever been given the operator's manual with the directions for how to successfully have one. We know the necessary ingredients: mutual respect, communications, negotiation, understanding differences, and, of course, romance and intimacy. But the puzzle remains—how do we put these elements into existence in our day-to-day relationships?

Finally, Dr. Chérie Carter-Scott has given us not only the rules, but also some clear instructions. *If Love Is a Game, These Are the Rules* is a delightful primer that clearly sets out the directions and the "care & feeding" guidance we need for keeping relationships healthy and alive. This handy and easily referenced book is full of bottom-line essentials, a map of the territory, that no one truly seeking love should go without. We see eye to eye regarding what couples need to help them develop and maintain authentic relationships. In many ways, her work is parallel to mine, and I consider her newest effort a perfect companion to my books, *Getting the Love You Want* and *Keeping the Love You Find*.

—Harville Hendrix, Ph.D.

Introduction

In 1998, *If Life Is a Game, These Are the Rules* was published, presenting the option of living life as a game in which you learn lessons from every experience, every day. That book was written to aid people along their personal path of discovery, growth, and development.

As seeking a partner is a natural part of the human experience, it made sense to focus this next book on love. *If Love Is a Game, These Are the Rules* offers the option of playing the game with a partner who plays by the same rules as you. It is one thing to play the game by yourself, but when you add a partner, learning opportunities multiply exponentially. With a partner in the equation, one and one equal three: your own experience, your partner's, and the experiences shared by the two of you. Entering the arena of love provides you and your partner with an entirely new set of lessons—lessons that can greatly enhance your lives.

Intimacy is a process in which two people pursue their own personal growth within the context of their relationship. Throughout the past 25 years, I have led workshops and facilitated couples in search of authentic relationships—those based on honesty, respect, communication, and a deep level of connection. I have assisted couples in defining their purpose, their expectations, their visions, their values, and their willingness to go beyond two separate entities of "I" and intentionally create a joint "we." I have witnessed unions being formed, formalized, and finalized.

Since I am also a lay minister, I have had the honor of officiating at dozens of ceremonies where the love of two people is officially proclaimed to the world. I have noticed how deeply both men and women long to share their lives. I have also witnessed how much effort, patience, and fortitude is required to make such relationships work. All these experiences, combined with my own life lessons, have taught me that love itself is natural and actually fairly easy; it is *relating* that presents the challenge.

Authentic love requires that you go deeper than the thrill of infatuation, beyond the rush of chemistry, and sometimes that you transcend the expectations of family, friends, and society. Authentic love requires that you discover and embrace your authentic self, and from that essential self draw to you the person with whom you want to hold hands and experience the adventure of life.

Yet what exactly is authentic love?

Authentic love is choosing your partner exactly as he is; it is putting your energy behind your choice and causing the relationship to be magical, rather than searching for reasons why it can't work. Love is supporting your partner in her choices, urging her to fulfill her heart's desires and go for all of her dreams.

Authentic love is honoring your partner's truth and wanting the very best for him. It is not controlling or possessing but rather respecting and trusting his unique path in life. Love is the courage to tell the truth especially when you believe it is unspeakable.

Authentic love means knowing your boundaries and respecting those of your partner; it means reaching out when you don't want to, communicating rather than assuming, and asking questions rather than jumping to conclusions. Authentic love means working things out rather than fighting, fighting rather than leaving, and staying through the misunderstandings, hurt feelings, and disappointments, knowing that through commitment all can be healed. It means staying when you want to give up, and honoring your commitment to work things out with the one you have chosen.

Authentic love means focusing on what you appreciate and why you are grateful. It means focusing on solutions rather than on problems. It means focusing attention on your partner and letting her know each day how much you care. It means treasuring your beloved and never taking her for granted.

Authentic love means living without judgments to create the safety to tell your truths. It means living each day with your partner as if it were your last. It is the willingness to be yourself and live in harmony with each other.

What does an authentic relationship look like? It looks and feels real. It thrives on honesty and shimmers with truth. An authentic relationship flexes and bends with the fluctuating needs and changes of each partner and gracefully weathers hardships. Both partners are committed to the growth and evolution of both individuals in their respective life paths. Much like the diamond used symbolically to represent the bond of matrimony, an authentic relationship sparkles with brilliance and light while maintaining a solid and enduring core. It is the context in which true love was meant to exist.

Of course, this is the ideal. The real fun—and opportunity—lies in reaching for such a vision. *If Love Is a Game, These Are the Rules* will give you the tools you need along the way as you learn how to win at love. Unlike any other "rules" book on love, these rules you don't need to study and learn. Rather, they are universal truths that you already inherently know in the depths of your being. You may have simply forgotten them when you fell under love's enchanting spell. Love can be a powerful force that sometimes eclipses reason and sound judgment. While the experience of new love is among the sweetest joys in life, it also presents a challenge: to remember the universal truths of how to relate while in the midst of your euphoria. I hope this book will aid you in that process.

I did not create these rules; they have existed since the beginning of time. My role is to present them to you, so that you may be reminded about the universal truths that guide love relationships into healthy, happy, and thriving unions. Rediscovering them will greatly help you in your journey to find, create, and sustain authentic and lasting love.

Whether you are in search of your soul mate or you want to make your existing relationship more intimate and connected, you will find here exactly what you need to answer your questions. Enjoy the journey!

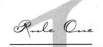

YOU MUST LOVE
YOURSELF FIRST

♥

*Your relationship with yourself is the central template from which
all others are formed. Loving yourself is a prerequisite to creating
a successful and authentic union with another.*

The relationship you have with yourself is the central relationship in your life. At the heart of all the elements that make up your life experience—family, friends, love relationships, work—is you. This is why a book about the rules of love begins with a rule not about relationships with others, but rather about the one you have with yourself.

There is a distinction between "you" and your "self." Your self is the core of your being, the essential entity that exists irrespective of your personality, your ego, your opinions, and your emotions. It is the small, sacred space within you that houses your spirit and soul. "You" are the observer, coach, editor, and critic who surveys your thoughts, words, feelings, and behaviors and determines how much of your essential self is shown to others.

The quality of the relationship between you and your self is paramount, for all your other relationships are based on it. This relationship acts as a template from which all the unions in your life are shaped, setting the quality, tone, and texture for how you relate to others and how they relate to you. It establishes the working model of how to give and receive love.

The depth and quality of the link between you and your self ultimately determines the success of your relationships with others. If an authentic love relationship is what you desire, then the first natural step you must take is to learn to love, honor, and cherish yourself as a truly precious and lovable being.

THE MISSING PUZZLE PIECE

Thousands of people have come to my personal growth workshops over the years to determine how they can find the love relationships they seek. I usually start by asking them to describe in detail how this person they seek would treat them, how they would feel around this partner, and how they would ideally want to relate. The responses, of course, vary from person to person, but several constants always surface: most say they want someone who is kind, considerate, and loving; who will treat them with respect and unconditional acceptance and listen to their wishes, goals, and dreams; who will make them feel special and cherished; who will cheer at their successes; someone with whom they can be open and honest and to whom they can feel completely connected in heart, mind, body, and soul.

When I ask these same people how many of these behaviors and actions they extend to themselves, most sheepishly admit that the answer is little to none. Many will acknowledge that they are critical of their flaws, override many of their needs, take for granted their positive attributes and accomplishments, and generally devote little time or attention to connecting with their own hearts and spirits. The same people who are seeking true love have little idea of how to offer it to themselves.

The place within you that generates self-love is the exact same place that attracts authentic love from others. If that source is clouded, your ability to attract a relationship that glistens with the magical sparkle of love is eclipsed. In order to bring light to that inner source, you will need first to learn how to give to yourself what you are seeking from another. Love creates more love, and when your own inner love light shines, you open yourself to experience the beautiful wonder of a deep and powerful connection with another being.

LEARNING TO LOVE YOURSELF

At its core, loving yourself simply means believing in your own essential worthiness. It is nurturing a healthy sense of positive self-regard and knowing in your heart that you are a valuable link in the universal chain. Loving yourself also means actively caring for every facet of yourself. It shows up in every action you take, from putting on a sweater to protect yourself from a chill to leaving a job that does not fulfill you. It means tuning in to your own wants and needs and honoring them the exact same way you want your partner to attend to you.

Not everyone grows up to have an innate sense of high self-esteem or worthiness. In fact, most of us need to work at it to some degree throughout our lifetimes. Each person feels insufficient in one or more areas, whether physical, intellectual, financial, or in interpersonal dynamics, emotional maturity, or spiritual growth. However, respecting, nurturing, honoring, and cherishing yourself is your birthright and something you can learn.

Loving yourself is the best way to learn *how* to love. Love is an action that requires certain understandings, skills, and capacities. By practicing loving with yourself, you train yourself to advance to the next level—loving another.

Only when you have successfully mastered taking care of your own needs can you know how to extend that same attention to others. When you respect the validity of your own thoughts and feelings, you can apply that consideration to others. When you believe within yourself how valuable you are, you can then bestow authentic affection on a partner.

If your objective is to play the game of love to win, then learning self-love is the first step you must take. Before you can roll the dice or even place your playing piece on the board, you need to tap into the inner reaches of your heart and soul and discover all that you are worth.

BEING A WHOLE PERSON

Love can do many things for you: it can bring you joy, help you grow, and expand you in ways you never imagined possible. Yet one thing love can never do is make you whole. You are the only one who can make yourself complete.

Many people have bought into the myth that there is someone out there who will serve as our "better half." This paradigm presumes that we are incomplete and require a partner to make us whole, and it feeds into what I call the "hole in the soul syndrome"—a core sense of insufficiency leading to feelings of emptiness, neediness, and self-reproach. Because of these feelings, we look for a partner to fill in the holes.

The grand irony is that the very sense of neediness that drives us to seek out love is exactly what will impede love from blossoming. Authentic love is attracted by those who desire it and is repelled by those who need it. Wanting connotes sufficiency and desire; needing connotes insufficiency and dependency. *I need* creates a vacuum effect that forces you to clutch, grab, cling, and consume; *I want* creates an openness that enables you to explore, consider, and shape the relationship you desire. It is only when you operate from the basis of being a whole person that you can find love based on *want* and not on *need*.

Victoria was raised in a household rich in luxury but devoid of affection. Her father was a very successful international business mogul who spent most of his time flying from one meeting to another, while her mother was preoccupied with her various charity events and social engagements. As a child, Victoria deeply longed for someone to notice her and lavish her with the attention she craved. She spent long hours alone in her bedroom, constructing elaborate fantasies about a famous musician who would write beautiful ballads declaring his undying love for her. She dreamed he would marry her and rescue her from her loneliness. She thought that once she found her beloved, she would no longer feel so empty inside and finally be happy.

As an adult, Victoria went from relationship to relationship, never able to find that idealized person who could quench her deep need for love. Her suitors stayed for brief periods but left with the same complaint: nothing they did ever seemed to be enough. Victoria was trapped in a cycle of seeking others to fill the hole in her soul. She became like an endless pit, insatiably draining her partners of their energy and vitality until they finally left, depleted. She would then immediately seek out another unsuspecting soul with whom she could repeat her pattern.

If you have personal development work to do in the area of self-love, as Victoria did, finding someone to love you is like trying to fill up a tank that has a hole in the bottom. No one can ever completely fill you up, because the leak will always create more need. No matter how much adoration, attention, and emotional support someone gives you, you will always need more—and more and more—because the love you receive from another can never replace the love you need to give yourself.

IMPRINTING INSTRUCTIONS FOR HOW TO LOVE YOU

If there is one basic law about the energy of love, it is this: *How you perceive and treat yourself is exactly how others will perceive and treat you.*

Every day you unconsciously show and tell people how to treat you without ever uttering a word. Since you are your own primary caretaker, others look to you for guidance on how much love you require. You give them the cues; you dictate how people speak to you, how they treat you, what they think of you, and what they expect from you. Whether you are conscious of doing this or not, you are the one who establishes the model of how others relate to you.

IMPRINTING NEGATIVE EXPECTATIONS

Ariella was a striking and tastefully dressed woman in her late 30s who came to me because she was, as she described herself, "cursed" when it came to relationships. When I suggested to Ariella that perhaps she was unconsciously manifesting her situations, she balked and waved my suggestion away. She insisted that her circumstances were a result of bad luck, so I sat back and asked her to tell me her story.

Ariella rarely dated, and when she did it was with either unavailable or inappropriate partners. She dated married men who could only give her scraps of time, men who were much younger and immature, or men who needed care taking—chemically dependent, in need of mothering, or trapped in emotional adolescence. Ariella relayed her tales of woe, complaining that fate did not want her to be happy or to find that special someone to love. She ended by declaring, "I guess I'll just be alone forever."

I asked Ariella some basic questions about herself, and almost immediately some core truths began to emerge. Ariella worked as a buyer for an upscale clothing boutique, a job that bored her; she stayed there because she didn't believe she could find a better position. She admitted that for a long time she had wanted to go to design school, but she had never taken the steps to make it happen. She rushed from one obligation to another and made little time for herself. She existed on diet soda, prepackaged food, and huge amounts of coffee, and she rarely engaged in any physical activity. In short, Ariella provided little to no nurturing for herself.

Ariella was surprised when I pointed out that the way she treated herself—with neglect, disrespect, and unkindness—was mirroring the way she was being treated by the men in her life. She never had to communicate how little she thought of herself; her self-concept was evident in her behavior. Her partners were simply responding to her message of how she should be treated.

THE BELIEF-RESULT CYCLE

I sensed that Ariella was starting to open up to this concept so I continued. I explained that our internal beliefs have two effects: first, they dictate our behavior, and second, they create an expectation in our own minds of how we deserve to be treated. Our behavior projects out to others, becoming the model of how to treat us; our unconscious expectation is transmitted on a more subtle level but with no less impact. Others respond to the model we project and the expectations we transmit; the result validates and reinforces our original belief.

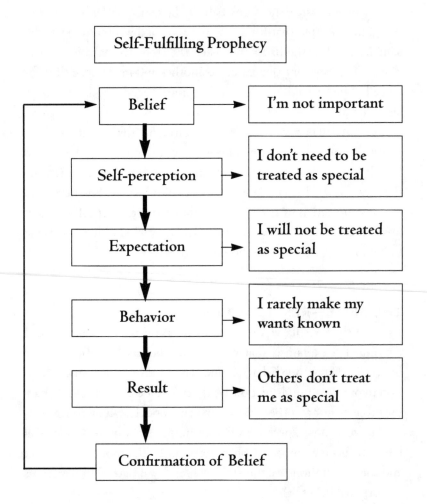

In Ariella's case, the cycle worked like this: Ariella had an unconscious belief about herself (I am not important). That belief dictated her behavior (I need not treat myself as special) and her expectation of how she deserved to be treated (I will not be treated by anyone else as special). Her behavior showed her partners how to treat her (I treat myself as unimportant, so you should also) and transmitted her expectations (I do not deserve or expect to be treated specially). As a result, she was not treated with respect, honor, or importance; her original negative belief was validated and reinforced.

As Ariella discovered, the laws of energy and attraction are impossible to circumvent. What you believe about yourself is projected outward into the world and becomes manifested in your relationships. It has been said that when people interview others for jobs, they are unconsciously drawn to those who are most like them. In the same way, when you interview for a mate, you are drawn to—and attract—those who treat you the way you treat yourself.

This essential piece of information was the key that unlocked Ariella's pattern of self-disdain and neglect. It allowed her to see that she needed to start with herself—to develop her own feelings of love and respect for herself before she could expect others to love and respect her.

This is not an easy concept to embrace, since it means accepting responsibility for what happens to you and who you attract into your life. Fortunately, the pattern of belief, behavior expectation, and result can be broken as soon as you become aware of it and adjust your beliefs about yourself.

If you believe you are unworthy of love, you will attract partners who treat you as if you are. If you treat yourself as unimportant, chances are you will be treated as such by your mate. If you are stingy with yourself, be it in terms of time, money, or attention, you will most likely attract a lover who lacks generosity toward you. If you do not take care of your physical self, your partner can hardly be expected to view your body as a temple. If you judge yourself harshly, then your mate will follow suit.

On the other hand, if you require respect, kindness, caring, and integrity in your relationship with yourself, you lay the groundwork to receive the same in your relationship with others. If you forgive yourself, others will know it is not acceptable to berate you for your mistakes. If you respect your needs, your partner will as well. If you listen to and honor your inner messages, your partner will respect your inner radar. Your internal beliefs and expectations will be reflected outward and you will be treated in kind.

SELF-ACCEPTANCE

One of the most important things you can learn from nurturing an authentic and loving relationship with yourself is acceptance. At the root of unconditional love is the perception that whatever your partner does, says, feels, or expresses will be received in an atmosphere free of condemnation. Practicing this kind of acceptance on yourself is what will enable you to extend that level of tolerance to your beloved.

If you accept your own imperfections, then you will be more tolerant of the imperfections of others. If you accept your mistakes, then you will be more forgiving of others' mistakes. If you learn from your own lessons, then you create room for others to learn around you.

ACCEPTING YOURSELF FIRST

Ben had a problem. He seemed to have no trouble finding and starting promising relationships, but he wasn't able to sustain them. After a few weeks of getting to know his latest relationship, Ben's "helicopter blades" began whirring in his head. He found fault with his partner's every action and mentally tore her to shreds. First she held the fork the wrong way, then she made too many grammatical errors, and next he found her laugh annoying. These perceived flaws became magnified to such an extent in his mental conversations, that sustaining any relationship was a major challenge.

Not surprisingly, Ben was less than forgiving of his own perceived flaws. I asked him to take one week and write down all the judgments he caught himself making about himself. At the end of that week, Ben showed me the list and admitted his shock to see how harshly he criticized himself. He had had no idea that he be-rated himself so, raining an endless array of judgments and criti-cisms on himself. It was no wonder Ben was intolerant of others' imperfections. Trained to seek out imperfections within himself, he automatically switched on the same mechanism toward his partners.

WHERE A LACK OF SELF-ACCEPTANCE LEADS

Lack of self-acceptance can go a long way toward eroding love rela-tionships with others, since the negativity you harbor about your-self will surely bleed onto your partner. Negativity is like a cancer that grows and spreads from one partner to the other, poisoning the entire relationship.

When Betsy married Nick, she knew that he had a small self-esteem problem. He often expressed insecurity about his abilities, but she was convinced that the power of her love would pull him out of it. Nick's self-esteem waxed and waned over the eight years they were together, until Betsy's professional life suddenly began to soar after years of hard work. Her catering business was written up in a national magazine and she received orders from all around the country. At that point, Nick began openly criticizing Betsy's work, calling her success a fluke and accusing Betsy of "thinking she was *so* important." His own insecurities reared up and manifested as an attack on his partner and her good fortune. Though Betsy tried to save their marriage with patience, communication, and finally therapy, the spiral of negativity and emotional assault continued until she finally left Nick to keep her own self-image intact.

At its extreme, low self-esteem can cause people to reject or sabotage love relationships almost automatically. Feelings of self-disdain and shame may run so deep that some people cannot allow anyone else to love them, no matter how much someone might try. They either cannot recognize authentic love, since they have no frame of reference to which they can compare their experience, or they reject their potential partner because they cannot imagine that anyone worth having would want them. While the old Groucho Marx joke about not wanting to be a member of any club that would have him for a member sounds amusing, there is a familiar ring to it. We all know people whose self-esteem is so low that anyone who cares about them comes under attack for just that. They are suspicious of anyone who shows interest in them because they, themselves, cannot find anything within themselves worthy of loving.

THE TOOLS FOR DEVELOPING SELF-LOVE

For most people, learning to love themselves is a lifelong process. It doesn't happen overnight or with the wave of a magic wand; rather, it needs to be developed and practiced daily, much as if you were learning a new sport. You need to learn the movements and then practice them again and again until they become as natural to you as breathing. Part of the beauty of living is that each person is given a lifetime to practice self-love.

You don't need to fully master self-love before you love another, but you do need to be actively on the path. There are countless resources you can turn to for guidance and encouragement; we are fortunate to live in a world and a time that encourages personal growth and self-awareness. Since the focus of this book is about relating and not specifically on building self-esteem, I will simply name a few of my favorite techniques for learning to love yourself and then encourage you to continue the journey on your own.

Loving yourself seems unspecific and abstract, so start by doing concrete tasks. For instance, each night write a list of "pats on the back." The list should start with the word "I" and list your accomplishments throughout the day. The items can be as minor as standing up to the dry cleaner when he ruined your favorite sweater, completing a project you delayed, or making a great pot of coffee; even small accomplishments can go a long way toward showing you your value. The purpose of this list is to shine your mental spotlight on the positive aspects to circumvent the automatic focus on the negative. In our workshops we say, "Ten acknowledgments a day keeps the 'beat-ups' away." It takes 21 repetitions of an action for it to become habitual; therefore, if you do this for 21 days in a row, you should notice a marked improvement in your level of self-confidence and self-perception. Your mind will no longer automatically seize upon all that you do wrong, but will instead shift over to what you, in fact, do right!

Another tool to create a context of self-care is the act of nurturing. This requires that you care for your relationship with yourself just as you would a relationship with a dear friend or loved one. Nurturing is a demonstration to yourself, from yourself, that you matter and that you are worth the expense of time, energy, effort, or money. Make a list of things that recharge and rejuvenate you; this can be anything from sensory pleasures to physical activity to spiritual practices that renew you. List only things that make you feel special. Things like:

> Watching the sunset
> Taking a bubble bath
> Having a massage
> Spending a day in bed when you're not sick
> Going biking
> Having coffee with a friend
> Eating a delicious treat
> Burning your favorite scented candle
> Meditating
> Listening to your favorite music

Choose at least one nurturing act per day and do it, even if you initially have to coax yourself. Soon you will learn to absorb nurturing, and the process of choosing and doing things on your list will become one of the highlights of your day.

Start with yourself. You have today. You have yourself. You have what it takes to love yourself. Start showing yourself and others how you should be treated, and soon you will understand the meaning of true, unconditional, and authentic love. From there, the wonderful experience of loving and being loved by another will be like a miraculous gift.

It matters not what tools you use to build your sense of self-worth. What matters is that you put forth the time and energy to learn to love the one person who will absolutely be with you for the rest of your life—yourself.

Rule Two

PARTNERING IS
A CHOICE

♥

The choice to be in a relationship is up to you. You have the ability
to attract your beloved and cause the relationship
you desire to happen.

*L*ove songs tell us that love is woven by the fingers of destiny.
From poetry we learn that love is an ever-elusive intangible that
wafts in like a wisp of smoke and disappears just as capriciously.
Friends may tell us that finding love is all about timing, yet bill-
boards imply that the secret to finding everlasting love is driving a
sexy car, wearing the right jeans, or having pearly-white teeth, fresh
breath, and great-smelling hair. It can be quite confusing.

Yet the real secret to finding authentic love lies not in your medicine cabinet, nor in the hands of fate or time. It resides in your own
consciousness.

What is your immediate response when I say "Finding love is up to you"? Do you believe you have the power within yourself to attract and find the kind of love you want? If you do, then by all means skip this rule and go on to Rule Three. If, however, any part of you thinks that finding love is not within your personal control or power, then you might want to read on a bit more.

Love does not "just happen." It needs to be created in much the same way you would create anything else. Let's imagine you wanted to make a meal. You might begin by thinking about what it is that you want to eat. Then you would assess how much time you have and what you could make within that period of time, decide what to make, take steps to secure the ingredients, follow the recipe, and then eat. You wouldn't just sit in your kitchen wishing a meal would somehow magically appear.

The process is not so different when it comes to love; love is also created from your imagination, intention, and deployment. Many mistakenly have thought that just *wanting* love is the same as *seeking* love. When my friend Alex was a child, she desperately wanted to make friends, but she was very shy and never went to any social events. Her mother always told her that she would never make friends sitting at home waiting for the party to come knock on her door. Now, at the age of 41, Alex is still sitting at home, waiting for her ideal mate. Not surprisingly, he still hasn't knocked. So there she waits, like many others, for the person to magically appear just like in the fairy tales, assuming they will then live happily ever after.

Unfortunately, it doesn't work like that. In order to create love in your life, you need to know what is required within yourself to start the process.

There are steps to take to turn the action of partnering from a faraway wish into reality. Taking these steps transforms your search for love from a game of chance into a conscious game of causality.

WHAT IT MEANS TO PARTNER

Before you proceed down the road of choosing to partner or not, it helps first to understand exactly what a true partnership is. A partnership is a union between two entities. Partnerships of any kind are formed when both people believe that greater benefit lies in uniting energies, talents, and resources than in remaining separate.

In the love arena, partnerships occur when two people come together to create a new reality. As both people move toward each other and connect in the physical, emotional, mental, and spiritual realms, they begin to move from separate "I" realities into a combined "we" reality, in which both "I's" contribute to the greater "we." Neither "I" is obliterated; both are simply augmented and enhanced by the chemical fusion with the other. Becoming a "we" reality means that you form a team whose intent is to travel through life together as a united force.

THE POSITIVES AND NEGATIVES OF PARTNERING

There are pros and cons to partnering. It can cause both positive and negative changes in your life and requires that you find ways to balance these polarities. The positive side is, of course, the hearts and flowers that you see in the movies and read about in romance novels. It is the wonderful rush of adrenaline that falling in love brings, the giddy feeling of being adored, the butterflies that flutter in your stomach when you hear your beloved's voice, and the warm rush of security you feel when he or she smiles at you from across a crowded room.

For most people, the main advantage is that you will no longer be alone, since you will have someone with whom you can spend your time and share the journey of life. Having a partner comes with some wonderful benefits: you have someone to love you, to give you attention, to take care of you, to act as your companion, to fulfill your sexual needs and desires, to do things with you, and to generally make life more fun. Partnering can provide support when you need it, encouragement when you are fearful, and empowerment when you have lost your belief in yourself. At its most elevated, a partnership can be a sacred bond in which you can share your innermost secrets, admit your weaknesses, grow in new and astonishing ways, and weave together your hopes and dreams.

The downside of partnering is the mirror opposite of its main benefit: You will no longer be alone. If you are no longer alone, that means you are also no longer *on your own.* You are no longer a stand-alone entity. You will need to deal with differences between you and your partner—in style, pace, modes of communicating, habits, and preferences. You have to deal with everyday life issues that accompany another person. Your partner, after all, has ideas, feelings, aspirations, habits, quirks, and issues that need to be given the same respect as you give your own. In other words, you need to make room in your life for another human being. When making choices and decisions, you will have to consider another person; you cannot just do whatever you want whenever you want without considering the other person's wishes. You will need to confer on everything from how much room you take up in the bed to how to spend your money. You must be willing to make adjustments so that both you and your partner can be happy.

Consider Gail, who took her daughter to an island resort and decided to look at a timeshare in a condominium complex for sale. They both fell in love with the unit, and Gail enthusiastically gave her credit card to make a down payment. She never paused to check with her new husband, Victor, since she had been so accustomed to being accountable only to herself for so many years. When Gail arrived home from the trip, however, she was confronted by Victor, who was angry that he wasn't considered on such a significant purchase and hurt that she had not consulted him. He let her know that her actions made him feel excluded and less than an integral part of their partnership.

Gail realized she had made a mistake and that she needed to

consider Victor's feelings and preferences as well as her own when making decisions that affected both of them. If the two of them were going to buy a vacation home to share, then both of their preferences—location, affordability, type of accommodation—needed to be taken into account.

Partnerships also demand that you be willing, at times, to change your plans to accommodate the other person's emergencies, needs, or wishes. In partnerships, you must give up some control, along with the need to always have your own way. While you were on your own, you were accustomed to doing whatever you wanted whenever you wanted. The appearance of a mate in your life suddenly changes all that. Having a partner adds a certain degree of complication and adjustment to your life for which you might not have bargained.

In order to create a partnership that succeeds, you will need to find ways to incorporate both the positive and the negative aspects. You will have to take the challenges with the harmony, the tests with the triumphs, and the issues with the inspiration. Partnership is essentially a package deal that cannot be chosen halfheartedly; it will require all your resources, willingness, and faculties to balance, and you will need the strength of your conviction to support you through the journey.

MAKING THE CHOICE TO PARTNER

Most of the world is designed for couples; that is just a fact of how our society is arranged. We expect people to travel through life in pairs, as though we are still preparing to board Noah's Ark, and we have built a world for two. We support romantic partnerships in thousands of ways, some subtle and others not so subtle, from giving tax breaks to married couples to creating a national holiday celebrating love and relationships. Some may opt for another type of relationship, which is not a partnership. Nevertheless, all of this creates expectations that we should *all* want and strive to find a partner and that being in a relationship is less a personal choice and more a mandate of society.

Frequently, my husband is unable to accompany me on business trips and from time to time I dine in restaurants alone. Each time I enter a restaurant alone and ask for a table, the maître d' peers at me and asks, "Just *one*?" Then, once I am seated, he or she will usually inquire if I want a magazine, silently inferring that my own company would be augmented by some stimulating literature. The assumption, of course, is that I have no one to share the moment with, and therefore dining alone must be a hardship. What makes me laugh about this is that it is not the lack of company that makes the experience a hardship, but rather the maître d's attitude!

So, too, do people believe that those traveling through life on their own are living a life of hardship. There is a certain amount of pressure to partner so that you will "fit in" and be able to follow the life path that conventional expectations dictate.

Yet this pressure can be dangerous, as so often relationships fall apart because one or both of the partners never viscerally chose to be in it in the first place. Perhaps they opted to partner because of family pressure or because they simply wanted to ease feelings of loneliness. But partnerships created from an external sense of *should* rather than an internal sense of *want* are usually unfulfilling. Finding a mate just so you don't disrupt paired seating arrangements at dinner parties is not a strong basis for an authentic union.

CHOOSING VERSUS DECIDING

In my last book, *If Life Is a Game, These Are the Rules,* I explained what happens when we take action based on reasoned decisions rather than visceral choices. The same model applies here, and I believe it is a key element to creating successful authentic relationships. The model is:

> *want* leads to *choice,* which leads to *commitment;*
> *should* leads to *decision,* which leads to *sacrifice.*

When you *choose* to partner, you make a conscious commitment to wanting a relationship. You intrinsically believe that you are ready and willing to be part of an authentic union. When you *decide* to partner, you may be thinking something like "Sure, why not?"

There is a degree of uncertainty about whether you truly want to partner, which quite often leads to unsatisfying results.

Where "Should" Leads

When I was 21, I was living with my college beau, Bill. My mother died that year, and my father informed my family shortly thereafter that he would be selling our family home and moving to Florida. I was upset because I had always had a fantasy about being married in my childhood home, so Bill and I rationally decided it would be as good a time as any to get married. From my perspective, Bill was charming, we were the best of friends, and he was an all-around great guy. All things considered, getting married seemed like the right thing to do at the time.

Over time, it became clear that we were not a match. We simply were not right for each other. While there was a warm camaraderie between us, there were no sparks or sizzle. We were more like brother and sister than lovers. We knew that in order to remain together, we both would have had to sacrifice our individual authenticity and our desire to be with someone about whom we felt deeply passionate—which neither of us wanted to do. Happily, the separation was amicable and he remains one of my dearest friends. I officiated at his wedding last year, and his new wife is truly aligned with what he needs in a partner.

Making the Choice Not to Partner

Sam was the only one of his peer group who was single. He was in his early 30s and, according to the world he was raised in, considerably behind schedule. No one could understand what had gone wrong, since Sam was handsome, intelligent, and fun to be with. Most of his friends already had one, if not two, children, and they joined his family in pressuring him to "settle down."

What his friends and family overlooked, however, was that Sam was in the middle of a career change that was occupying all his time and attention. He knew that he wanted to feel secure in his career before he embarked on a committed, lifelong relationship, and so he made the conscious choice to postpone marriage until he was set in his career path.

When I asked Sam how he felt about all this, he rolled his eyes good-naturedly and said, "What no one seems to understand is that it's not that I'm afraid of commitment, or marriage, or anything like that. I've met women along the way that I might have considered marrying, but I never did because I knew in my gut that I just wasn't ready yet. As soon as I am ready and I meet the right person, I'll let everyone know!"

I found Sam's perspective refreshing. It's hard to feel different from your peer group. It requires an inner strength to withstand family pressure and to hold firm to your inner convictions about what is right for you. Sam knew instinctively what so many people take years to learn: that everyone is on his own life path and timetable, and that choosing a lifelong partner is a shift that must come from within your deepest self if the union is to be an authentic one.

IS PARTNERING WHAT YOU WANT?

Partnering is not for everyone. Ideally, it is for those who want to grow through and with another person, who are ready to embark on the journey of combining the various elements of their life with someone else's. For some, partnering is an obvious and desirable choice. For others, it is a choice that they are either still considering or that they know is not for them at this stage in their life.

There is a difference between saying you choose to partner and really truly feeling that way. Simply to speak the words is not enough. You will need to know whether the words are a reflection of your most basic inner truth. If they are, then your willingness is absolute. If they are not, your inner hesitancy will show up in tangible results. If you are unclear whether you want to partner or not, or you want to be certain that your willingness is genuine, ask yourself these questions:

> When I consider being in a relationship, what reaction comes up?
> Am I willing to move beyond my existing comfort zone of emotional exploration?

Do I want to share my time (or space, money, etc.) with
    someone?
Am I willing to make adjustments and concessions?
Am I prepared to make communicating a priority?

If your inner knowing leads you to see that you are not ready, or
do not want, to partner, then you will be able to speak your truth to
others in a way that will help them respect your position. When
Sam's friends and family continued to press him about his single
state, he eventually told them all quite firmly that he was happy the
way he was and would let them know when he was involved in a significant relationship. They backed off. Although his mother still
asks now and then if he's dating anyone, and his friends poke good-
natured fun at him, they have ceased their aggressive barrage of un-
invited opinions and nosy inquiries about his status.

If you fully understand what it means to partner and you choose
in your heart to seek out that experience, then you have taken the
first essential step on what I believe will be the most exciting and
fulfilling journey of your lifetime. Of course, I am partial to love
relationships, or else I would not be writing an entire book about
them. I believe that authentic love can be the shining jewel in your
crown and the source of your greatest joy in life. Finding it may require some work, but it is well worth the effort.

Making the conscious *choice* to partner greatly increases your
chances of finding a true and authentic union. When you choose
from that inner-centered place within you that dictates what you

know to be right for you, you alert the universe that you are ready for an authentic and meaningful partnership and you are led toward situations that are aligned with your intentions.

The willingness that is created as a result of your inner choice is what enables you to begin playing the game of love. It moves you to the "Go" square so that you can start rolling the dice and moving around the board. Your choice of "yes" releases an energy within you—and around you—that will propel you forward and sustain you in your search for true love.

TAKING ACTION

Let's say you have made the choice that you want to find and embark on an authentic relationship. You know in your heart that you are prepared for all that such a union will offer, both positive and negative, and are ready to move forward. Now what?

These are steps you can take to bring an authentic love partner into your life:

1. Know what you want.
2. Create your vision.
3. Recognize what might be in your way.
4. Manifest your intention.

Can I guarantee that by following these steps you will manifest the love of your dreams? No, but I can tell you that the success rate I've witnessed for this is very high, and chances are very good that the steps will lead you toward the authentic relationship you are looking for.

STEP ONE: KNOW WHAT YOU WANT

You can't get what you want unless you know what it is. Without knowing what it is that you want, you might get *something,* but you will then have to simply want what you get.

If you know what you want in a relationship but have no sense of what that partner would be like, then you will need to go through quite a few people until you are able to assess what you *don't* want in order to figure out what you do. This is probably not the most satisfying way to find love; in fact, it sounds fairly exhausting. I know a man who has dated countless women in the past year and is still unsure about exactly what he is looking for. He could save a lot of time if he just knew what he wanted.

There is a faster and more fluid route to finding the mate you want other than dating and discarding dozens of potential partners. It begins with an inner assessment of who you are, what you are about, and, yes, what it is that you truly want.

Knowing Yourself

Getting to know yourself is the first part of this process. To know who you are means you are connected to your essence. It means you understand what makes your heart sing, what brings you joy, what makes you angry, what situations are and are not right for you, and what you will and will not tolerate. It means you are aware of your internal filters, issues, and beliefs and you can recognize what expectations you bring to relationships. It means you can align yourself with your desired life path, rather than following innumerable bunny trails that lead to nowhere.

When you are in sync with yourself, then you can know what you will need to have in a partner and a relationship in order for it to feel authentic to you. It is only with self-knowledge that you can make a wise choice about the person who will ultimately be compatible with you. The more you know and understand yourself, the greater your chances for success in your relationship. Use this as motivation to do a thorough assessment of yourself. Your goal is to be true to yourself so that you can find a loved one who will be true to you, as well.

To know and understand yourself is not very difficult, but the process does take an investment of time and energy. You can discover things about yourself through reading, talking, making lists, writing a journal, meditating, praying, taking workshops or classes, going on vision quests, seeing a therapist, an astrologer, personal coach, or any other guide. You then choose to find out about

yourself, your tolerances, your passions, your proclivities, your pho-
bias, and your requirements for satisfaction. Whatever vehicle you
choose to learn about yourself should provide you with the essential information from which to grow and connect to another.

Knowing What You Want in a Mate

Once you have a good sense of who you are, the next part of this
step is to assess what type of person is the right match for you.
Asking the universe for someone to love without giving any specifi-
cations is like walking into a restaurant and asking for food. The
chances of the wrong thing being served are quite high, since there
really was no right thing to begin with. You can keep asking for
something wonderful, but the definition of wonderful is subjective.
You need to be specific and clear, and articulate your desires so you
can receive exactly what you want.

As a teenager, Ginger was very clear about her criteria for a
boyfriend. He needed to be handsome, well dressed, popular, and a
good kisser. It was a bonus if he drove the right car, but not required. As she matured, she never revisited her teenage criteria, and
found it difficult to connect with any of the men she was attracting,
all of whom fit her original criteria. She found herself in her mid-
20s running down her checklist from childhood with yet another
new candidate. When he didn't match up with her standards, as so
few of the men she met did, she was immediately ready to discard
him. This time, however, she stopped herself and thought, "Maybe

my criteria are outdated. I've never revised my list; maybe I need a new one."

Ginger thought about it and came up with what seemed like her mother's list: a good provider, a good husband, a good father, a churchgoer, a wise investor, one who saves money, and so on. She looked at the list and thought: "This is my mother speaking, not me. What do *I* want?" It was time for her to articulate her adult list, but she had to give it some thought.

As it turned out, Ginger's new list was quite different from her teenage list and her mother's. Her new list started out with: co-adventurer in life, then went on to honorable, kind, good sense of humor, willing to do activities in cutoffs one day and dinner jacket the next, good communicator and partner. She was amazed at how she had changed and how clear she was about what she wanted after just a short time sorting it out.

Listing Your Criteria

The best way to clarify what you want in a mate is by making a list of your criteria. Writing your criteria down allows you to become conscious of what you are looking for. Many people have a vague sense of what they want, but writing it down makes it concrete. If you create this list from your true self, you will be better prepared to avoid the pitfalls of letting hormones or infatuation entice you to enter into or stay in a relationship with someone who is not going to be the right match for you.

Ideally, your list would consist of three parts. The first part contains those essential requirements that are nonnegotiable—your "must have" criteria. These are the qualities, preferences, behaviors, abilities, attitudes, beliefs, and hobbies that you want embodied in your beloved, that you cannot live without in a partner. For example, Kim, a playful 31-year-old with an upbeat and mischievous nature, finds laughter among her greatest joys in life. For her, a sense of humor is essential in a partner. She knows that in order to be happy, she needs someone who knows how to have fun.

The second part is your negotiable wish list. These are the qualities that are not essential but would be preferable in your ideal mate. For example, Mack, who is an avid scuba diver, put "likes to scuba dive" on his wish list. He would not reject someone because she didn't like to dive, but in his perfect world, he would find a veritable mermaid with whom to explore the depths of the sea.

The third part of your list details the unacceptable, nonnegotiable aspects, or what I call the "knockout punch" list. For some, a knockout punch would be an alcohol or drug addiction. For others, it might be someone with a nasty temper. For someone like Bonnie, who very much wants to be a mother someday, it is someone who does not want to have children. She knows she would not pursue a relationship with a man who does not want to have a family. Each person has his or her own boundaries of what will absolutely not work for him or her; only you know what is true for you.

Your list will help you become clear on what you want in a mate.

It will enable you to get your criteria out of your head and into tangible form, so that you can bring the fog of "what I *think* I want" into a focused vision of "what I *know* I want." You create real standards and qualifications for the position of "my partner," which will prevent you from trying to fit every person who comes along into that role. Put this list away in a drawer or some safe place so that you can refer to it when a potential partner appears in your life.

A Sample List

Recently, a woman in her early 30s named Jennifer came to my workshop to create her relationship criteria list. The list Jennifer created contained some of the most well-thought-out criteria I had ever seen, and I would like to share it with you as an inspiring example. Of course, your criteria may be completely different; I offer you Jennifer's list simply to start you thinking about what might be true for you.

JENNIFER'S LIST

Must Haves

1. Someone smart and intellectually stimulating, who is compatible with me in that he likes to talk about ideas.

2. Someone spiritual or interested in developing himself and a spiritual life.

3. A good person with a big heart, who is kind and loving.
4. Someone who takes care of his professional and financial life.
5. Someone who is committed to the relationship, who is willing to work on it.
6. Someone who is supportive of my goals and dreams and can be supportive when I am having a rough time or a bad day. Someone who is willing to take support from me in return, who won't hide or run away when he needs support.
7. Someone who is passionate and has a zest for life.
8. Someone who isn't fooled by my self-reliance and can see and accept my vulnerability.
9. Someone with a strong sense of integrity.
10. Someone who wants to be a father someday.

Wish List

1. Someone who likes to travel.
2. Someone who likes to read and see movies.
3. Someone who makes me laugh.
4. Someone who enjoys entertaining.
5. Someone who gets along with my friends.
6. A good lover who can express himself physically and lovingly with consideration and openness.
7. Tall—at least taller than I am.

Knockout Punches

1. Someone who is unwilling to be open and communicative, who withdraws when problems arise.
2. Someone who lives far away—who would be a long-distance relationship.
3. Someone who has a history of infidelity.
4. Someone who does not like my family, or whom my family does not like.
5. Someone who does not value or maintain his friendships.
6. Someone to whom I am not physically attracted.

Jennifer is still "interviewing" for the right mate, and she frequently refers to her list whenever she feels tempted to begin a new relationship out of desperation or loneliness or intense physical attraction. Her list enables her to pause and assess each new man she meets and to say no to those candidates who are not right for her, so she can leave a space vacant for the right person when he does show up.

Having created your own list and the image in your mind of your ideal mate, you are ready to proceed to the second step: creating your vision of the relationship that you desire.

STEP TWO: CREATE YOUR VISION

Just as you created your vision of your ideal mate, so, too, must you create your vision of your ideal relationship so that you know what you are looking for. The vision you create then becomes your barometer for compatibility. You will know when someone comes close enough to qualify as "the one."

To lay out your vision, you first need to know the dynamics of the relationship you want. For example, Mel knows he is looking for a traditional arrangement in which he and his partner get married, have children, and move to a house in the suburbs. He would not mesh with Kathleen, who is looking for someone who would be comfortable living together and does not necessarily ever want to legally consummate the partnership. Sherry is looking for what she calls "the best friend model," which she perceives as someone who would be her best mate, closest companion, and with whom she would share activities. Joel, on the other hand, wants someone who will understand how demanding his work is and will accommodate him. Marci wants someone she can "hang out with," while Robert is looking for a wife who can help him entertain his many business associates and clients. None of these relationship models are better or worse; each is simply a reflection of what that person envisions to be right for him or her.

Factors to Consider

There are many factors to consider when laying out your vision. To begin with, there is the connection between you and your ideal partner. Are you looking for a close, intimate relationship, as Sherry is, or do you want one with more space, like Joel? How accountable do you want to be to your partner, and she to you? How do you want to relate to each other?

Next, there are lifestyle issues to consider. Where would you live? What style would you live in? What kind of social life would you have? What activities would you do together? Would you travel?

Life path issues are of course important. Do you want children? How many? When? Do you plan to retire by a certain age, and if so, what do you plan to do? Do you envision your partner doing this with you?

All of these things matter in terms of compatibility. Put these in the drawer next to your vision of what you want in a mate, so that you can have your criteria in a safe place when you do meet someone and begin to evaluate whether she is the one for you. When you do find a potential partner and embark on a relationship, these issues then become ideals to disclose and negotiate.

STEP THREE: RECOGNIZE WHAT MIGHT
BE IN YOUR WAY

You know who you are. You know what you want in a mate. You have created the vision of your ideal relationship. Now comes the hard part: finding and rooting out the issues that might be standing in your way.

If your immediate response to this is "The only thing in the way is the fact that I just can't find the right person," then I would like to refer you back to the section in Rule One about the effect our beliefs have on our behaviors, expectations, and results. I would also like to tell you that what stands in your way is your belief that you cannot find or have what you are looking for.

Unconscious Beliefs

Unconscious beliefs are very powerful. There is a popular psychological notion that says, "If you think you can or think you can't, either way, you're right." This notion describes what is known as a self-fulfilling prophecy. It means that you approach a situation with certain assumptions, beliefs, and perceptions so that what you believe to be true has a tendency to manifest.

For example, my friends Matthew and Andrea, a married couple, live right outside of Denver. Recently, I went to Denver to work on a project and stayed with them for an extended period of time. I frequently drove into the city with one of them while the other stayed home.

When I drove in with Matthew, we always found a parking space. Someone was always just pulling out as we approached; it seemed so easy. Each time, he remarked, "It's so easy to find parking spaces in the city," and he was right.

Andrea, on the other hand, became tense as soon as we approached the city limits. "You can never find a parking space in the city," she would complain. "There are just too many people and too many cars. It's impossible." And you know what? She was right. Often Andrea and I drove around for 45 minutes without finding one available space.

I found it curious and fascinating that both of them were right about the same reality in the same city even though they had diametrically opposite views. Needless to say, I always tried to arrange my schedule so that I traveled into the city with Matthew instead of Andrea. Who wants to spend 45 minutes looking for no place to park?

Similarly, if you set out to find love believing it is not available to you or that you can't make it work, then that is what you will find. Take some time to examine your beliefs to see if they are aligned with your desired outcome. You can waste a lot of time doing diligence for a task that you don't really believe is possible in the first place.

Inner Hesitancy

If so many people want to find love, why is there such a discrepancy between what they say they want and what they actually have in their lives? For many people, there are hidden blocks to finding love that create what I call the "external yes, internal no" syndrome. When there is a gap between what you say you want and what you get, there is something subtle and unconscious within you that is responding "No" to the question of your willingness to partner.

These hidden obstacles lurk in the subconscious mind, preventing the manifestation of the love we say we desire. When you feel tripped up in the process of attracting and sustaining authentic love, it is worth a moment to pause and search the innermost pockets of your heart, mind, and soul for any beliefs, fears, concerns, or doubts that may be blocking love from freely flowing to you. These obstacles do not determine your destiny, nor do they dictate your success or failure at the game of love. Rather, they are merely hurdles to overcome so that you can turn your desire for an authentic relationship into reality.

Fear of Getting Hurt

Trix's unconscious block was the fear of getting hurt. For many years she had been in an abusive marriage, but eventually she had found the courage and the strength to leave. After giving herself a year to heal, she began to date again, but she kept finding herself drawn to men who were not available for one reason or another—

one was emotionally shut down, another was unwilling to commit, another was gay. She was demoralized.

After Trix started to recognize a pattern, we talked. I asked her if there could possibly be something in the way. At first, she had no response. It was clear to her that she wanted to be in a healthy relationship and none of the right men were forthcoming.

I probed a little deeper: "Do you have any thoughts, images, or fears that might unconsciously be putting on the brakes?"

As she looked straight into my eyes, tears began rolling down her cheeks. "Yes," she whispered. "I'm so afraid of being hurt again. I don't want to ever relive that horror."

"Perhaps," I commented, "part of you is saying 'Yes' at the same time another part is saying 'No.' You probably send the message, 'Come closer, but not too close; go away, but not too far.' Men who receive your message are most likely confused by the mixed signals."

Once Trix rooted out the fear that was blocking her way, she was able to get closer to the belief that love did not necessarily lead to pain. When she acknowledged and articulated her fears, they lifted, as fears tend to do when we shed light on them. Soon, a legitimate candidate showed up professing undying love for her. She was amazed and delighted.

For many people, fear of getting hurt prohibits them from finding the love they are seeking. They may say they want love, but what they really want is *guaranteed* love. Ask yourself: Am I looking for a relationship or a money-back guarantee for my emotions?

Fear of Losing Love

George was afraid that if he found love, he would be unable to sustain it. When I met him, George had a bad track record. Relationships were not his strong suit. He was a pilot and knew very well how to fly planes, but when it came to women, that was another matter. Janice, a flight attendant, suggested he come and see me.

"I just don't think I have anything to offer," he said. "I travel all the time, and when I'm home I'm either sleeping, training pilots, or fishing. That's no life for a relationship." I asked him what he wanted and he said that he would dearly love to have a mate, a companion, a best friend, and a lover, but things never worked out for him. I asked him if he was afraid of anything. He said, "With all of the divorces, the odds for success are very slim. I know people who are much better communicators whose marriages have ended in divorce. I don't stand a chance."

I asked George if he could speak honestly about his fears with someone he was involved with. He thought it was possible. "If you can honestly state your considerations and fears to your love and ask for her support," I told him, "I think you have a good chance of success. Now go out there and prove me right." It took more than a year for George to find his special someone, but it did happen. He sent me a postcard from Turkey that read, "We're together. She loves to travel, and when I talk, she listens. It's working! Thanks a million. George."

It has been two years since I received that postcard, and George and his lady are still very happily together. Despite his original concerns, George was able to sustain a relationship and keep the wonderful love he found.

Is fear of losing love preventing you from finding it in the first place? If it is, you will need to search inside to find the courage to take a chance. With every new love comes risk, and you can only reap the rewards if you overcome your fear and give the person—and yourself—a chance.

Setting Unreachable Standards

Setting unrealistically high expectations for a partner is another possible deterrent that stems from fear. If you set unreachable standards, you will never have to risk getting hurt, because you will never find anyone. This is what I encountered in a conversation with Roger.

When Roger described his ideal woman, I noticed that he wanted a series of different fantasy women all rolled into one. He wanted this woman to have the figure of Barbie, the power of Xena, and the sweetness of Dorothy from *The Wizard of Oz*. She must be as demure and charming as Princess Diana, as sexual as a Playboy Bunny, and as intelligent as Barbara Walters. She should be pleasant, agreeable, easy to get along with, but very interesting to converse with.

I candidly asked him if he saw himself as James Bond. He laughed and said, "No." I asked him if he was looking for the perfect woman, to which he replied, "Yeah. Sounds impossible, right?"

I explained to Roger that there was a difference between

envisioning your ideal mate and envisioning a superhuman one. By setting his expectations so high, he was preventing himself from ever engaging in any real relating, since no one person could ever fit his criteria.

Are your criteria realistic? If your description of your ideal mate sounds more like Superman or Wonder Woman than a human, you may want to assess whether you are setting unreachable standards just so you can prove to yourself that there is no one out there for you.

Establishing Limited Parameters

Joy's situation was not so different from Roger's in that she was preventing herself from finding a good relationship by setting limited parameters. Joy would only date dark-haired, physically fit lawyers or doctors between the ages of 35 and 40 who lived on the Upper East Side of Manhattan. There are only so many men who fit these criteria, and when Joy finally dated and discarded all the men in this category, she declared her situation hopeless. I suggested to Joy that her range of requirements was a bit narrow, and that perhaps she should look inside herself again and be absolutely certain she wanted to find someone to partner with.

Joy took my advice and finally realized that she was afraid of finding someone because, in her mind, it would mean giving up her independence. She liked answering to no one but herself, and realized that she had a ways to go before she could answer "Yes" to fully being in a relationship with someone.

Are your parameters too narrow? If you think you have already dated everyone who fits your criteria, then perhaps they are. Ask yourself what you have invested in not allowing yourself to venture outside your small definition of what is desirable; you might be surprised to discover that it might be a lack of willingness that is preventing you from relaxing some old rigid expectations.

It is so easy to blame external circumstances or fate for your inability to manifest the love you want. Yet almost always the cause of unrealized dreams of love stems from within us. All you need to do is look within and ask yourself, How willing am I really to partner?

STEP FOUR: MANIFEST YOUR INTENTION

Manifesting is the act of bringing into tangible existence something that has been a dream, wish, or goal. It is focusing your intention on a specific and defined outcome and then causing that intention to be realized.

In its purest energetic sense, manifesting occurs as a result of magnetically drawing to you that which you desire. By putting forth your intention into the universe, you are setting the energy wheels in motion so that you may receive exactly what you requested.

Manifesting your ideal mate does require a dash of wizardry, but it is not as hocus-pocus as it sounds. There are times when simply putting forth your intention is enough to yield results, but more often than not you will need to combine that intention with real, tangible efforts in order to yield the desired outcome. There will even be times when the combination of intention and effort is not quite enough; then you will need to bring in the heavy artillery of "doing whatever it takes."

Imagine if you wanted to find a new job. While playing tennis, your friend mentions that he knows someone who is searching for someone just like you. Voilà! You manifested a job through intention alone.

Now let us suppose that finding a job is bit more challenging. You would still put forth your intention, this time combined with effort. You might start by telling people you know that you are looking for a job, looking in the help-wanted section of the classifieds, and sending out some resumes. If a job shows up through such measures, then you manifested it through intention plus effort.

Now let us suppose that some time has elapsed and no job has surfaced. You would then continue to put forth your intention and effort, but you also need to move into "doing whatever it takes" mode. This is when you go above and beyond to bring about your desired results. You might take an internship to gain experience in your desired new field, or see a career coach for guidance, or contact headhunters. In other words, you pull out all the stops to realize your goal. When a job shows up through these measures (as it usually does, unless there is some hidden internal obstacle in your way), then you manifested it through intention plus effort plus whatever else was needed.

The process is the same when you are looking for the right

relationship. Jodi is the perfect example of someone who manifested her beloved through intention alone. She mentioned to her friend Evelyn that she was ready to find the right person, and Evelyn responded that she had someone wonderful with whom to arrange a blind date. The moment Jodi opened the door and laid eyes on Scott, she felt an instant connection. They were married last year.

For Rosemary, on the other hand, a little more effort was required. She made her criteria list and casually let her friends know she was looking to meet someone new. When no candidates automatically surfaced, she started going out to parties and other social functions where she might meet someone. She met a few possible candidates, but none of them panned out. After almost a year, she was growing frustrated, but she persevered in her efforts and forced herself to continue going out to parties, charity events, and cultural experiences at her favorite museum. She eventually met Jeffrey at a black-tie fund-raiser and was delighted to see how many of her criteria he met.

For Julie, the search required a move into doing whatever it takes. Her previous intention and effort yielded only disappointing dates and sputtered beginnings, so she stepped up her efforts to a higher level. She enrolled in a highly respected dating service to increase her chances of meeting her ideal mate. After a few months of dating, she went to a singles vacation resort and met Brian, who fulfilled all of her must haves and a high percentage of her wish list. They connected and are still together years later.

WHEN MANIFESTING DOESN'T WORK

Sometimes there are trials and errors. Manifesting doesn't always work the first time. If you repeat the process many times with no success, it is helpful to take a step back and reexamine whether there are any hidden obstacles in your way. I truly believe, as my experience has taught me, that there is no such thing as impossible when it comes to manifesting a realistic goal. If you are truly putting forth all your intention and effort and not finding what you want, then the resistance is probably coming from within you, not from the universe. Go back; look within, revise, assess, edit as necessary. Eventually, you *will* find the love you are seeking.

Manifesting takes intention, time, patience, and sometimes real effort. The key is to trust the process and have faith that the love you want and deserve will flow to you as it should.

When you have made the conscious choice that a union is what you want and you follow the steps to partnering, the laws of energy are on your side. The result of your inner examinations and manifesting efforts will produce potential partners, one of whom will be the love you are seeking. Then you will have begun the process of creating an authentic relationship.

Rule Three

CREATING LOVE
IS A PROCESS

♥

*Moving from "I" to "we" requires a shift in perspective and
energy. Being an authentic couple is an evolution.*

The evolution of true love is a process that begins with the
creation of a "we" reality. When both partners merge their "I" into
the greater "we," they shift the way they perceive their life and circumstances. They do more than simply touch the edges of their
lives together. Rather, they weave their interpersonal threads together to form a new fabric.

Authentic love is built on a foundation of strong, intimate
bonds that can only be formed through time and experience. Imagine if you tried to build a house without taking the time to be sure

each board and stone was properly placed and supported and every nail hammered in securely. The house might actually be built in record time, but at what cost? How well would you sleep at night when a storm was raging around your hastily built structure?

It is the same with relationships. Think of your relationship as the house you are building and the process of creating love as the work that goes into building it. If you try to rush through the stages of creating authentic love, you may end up with something that looks like a relationship but may not be secure enough to sustain you through life's stormy times.

TRUST THE PROCESS

Forming a couple is not all that difficult; anyone can link up with another person and declare themselves coupled. It is forming an *authentic* union that poses the challenge. This challenge can only be met by respecting the process of its creation and its natural evolution.

When we first encounter a potential partner, we may be tempted to rush the process so that we can get through the evolutionary stages quickly and get to the "good stuff." However, love is an energy with inherent laws, and one of them is that love refuses to be rushed.

A LESSON IN PATIENCE: DONNA AND DAVID

Donna and David met at a party. The attraction was immediate, and after spending the majority of the evening sequestered in a private corner talking, David asked Donna out for a date the following night. She happily agreed, since David was one of the most handsome and exciting men Donna had ever met.

As Donna left the party, the hostess, who was also a friend of David's, cautioned her. She warned Donna that David had a reputation for coming on strong and then later disappearing. Donna thanked her friend for her concern, but dismissed her words as she floated out the door, anticipating what she would wear the following evening. She could hardly wait.

By the end of their first date, David told Donna she was the woman he had been looking for his entire life. Donna was so enraptured that she blocked out the little voice in her head that echoed her friend's words and suggested that perhaps she should take her time and get to know David a little better before leaping into a relationship with him. She knew she should probably let things build over time, but the whirlwind was too exciting to relinquish. She had been waiting for someone like David for so long that she didn't want to mess things up by applying the brakes.

Donna and David fell into an exclusive relationship almost immediately. To Donna, David was perfect. He fit all her surface requirements for the perfect mate: he was handsome, successful at a high-profile and glamorous job, of the same religious background as she, and a considerate lover. She tried not to worry too much about the other details, assuming they would get to know each other over time.

They never did get to know each other. As time passed, Donna discovered that David was unwilling to share any part of himself with her other than what she saw in those first few weeks. She grew frustrated as David continued to deflect her questions about his life philosophy, his hopes, dreams, values, goals, or his past. Whenever Donna tried to take their relationship a bit deeper, he withdrew. David continued to pull back until he finally lived up to his reputation and dropped Donna by sending her a good-bye E-mail and then disappearing from her life. She was devastated.

It took Donna many months to get over David. As the pain began to subside, Donna was able to finally see that she never really knew David at all. She had rushed the process with him because she so desperately wanted to be in a relationship. Like so many people do, she was so swept away with the *idea* of love that she didn't take the time to make sure David was the right person for her. As a result, there were no bonds of intimacy built between them other than those spun out of fantasy and hope. She saw in hindsight how glossing over any misgivings she had about David and careening into a relationship with him had set her up for heartbreak.

When I asked Donna a few years later about that experience, she gave a bittersweet laugh and surmised that almost everyone has made that mistake at least once. I agreed. As humans, we feel the need for love so deeply that we sometimes allow our instincts and reason to be eclipsed by passion and hope. Although we know in our rational minds how essential it is to really get to know someone before opening our hearts and making rash decisions about our future, so many of us plunge ahead in our rush to have our dreams fulfilled.

The only way out of this trap is by learning the lesson of patience. If your desire to be in love is taking precedence over your desire to be in love with the right person, you may find yourself grasping at any available candidate who comes along, usually with disappointing ends. Trying to rush love is as futile as trying to rush time; each must evolve as it was meant to. This is not an easy lesson to learn, but learn it you must if your desire is for a truly authentic relationship.

The key to creating authentic love is to trust the process. Millions of couples have proved that it works. It may not happen overnight, but if you have patience and perseverance, love will reward you with its astonishing and wondrous gifts.

THE STAGES OF LOVE

The stages of love are really quite simple. There are five of them, beginning from the moment you and your partner meet and extending to the moment that you and your partner mutually and consciously choose to form a new entity—the "we" reality. In order, they are connection, exploration, evaluation, building intimacy, and commitment.

STAGE ONE: CONNECTION

Connection occurs when the exchange of energy between two people flows without reservation. Romantic connections usually begin with a spark—that invisible chemical attraction that draws two people together like magnets. Sometimes it feels like déjà vu, that strange familiarity as though you have known that person before; it can also show up as an intense feeling of stimulation, or as a sense of profound comfort. Though seemingly small, that initial spark is what illuminates the doorway to love's higher realms.

Many people immediately think of a physical attraction when they define connection. After all, chemistry can be very powerful. When we meet someone with whom there is a sexual attraction, our hearts beat faster, our bodies flush, our imaginations race, and we may suddenly feel as though we are somehow cosmically linked to this fascinating creature before us.

Connection can occur on several different levels, often at the same time: mentally, when two minds "click"; emotionally, when two personalities are "simpatico"; or spiritually, when two souls vibrate at the same frequency.

Every couple has a story about their initial connection. Barry claims he knew he was going to marry Camille the moment he laid eyes on her, when she opened the door and greeted him for their blind date. Rachel and Tom (both *Star Trek* fans) experienced what they refer to as their "mind meld" the night they met at a friend's apartment. Eric and Stephanie spent the entire evening laughing together when they met at a Halloween party. The only universal and defining point I can make about connection is that you know it when it happens.

A word of caution, however: A strong connection is not the same thing as being in love, nor does it automatically mean you are meant for each other. Connection is important between any two people who want to pursue a relationship, but it is only the first step. You can connect with many people over the course of your lifetime, but it is only by following through on the rest of the steps that you can know if this is truly the love of your life.

STAGE TWO: EXPLORATION

Exploration is the "getting to know you" phase, characterized by endless hours spent talking on the phone deep into the night, long walks in the park talking about childhood memories, and romantic dinners revealing secret wishes and dreams. Both people reveal their personal histories and share their stories. With each new piece of information, layers are peeled back, and the couple draws closer to each other's core essence.

The exploration stage is important because this is when you find out the information you will need to assess whether your new partner will ultimately be compatible with you. If the exploration process is rushed or overlooked, as it was with Donna and David, you may find yourself with someone who you either do not really know or who is not right for you.

Peering over the Rose-Colored Glasses

This stage can often be colored by the first blush of romance. In the midst of learning all the wonderful new things about your partner and the exhilaration of revealing your innermost thoughts, it can be a challenge remembering to proceed with your eyes open and your antennae tuned. Though it may be tempting to keep the rose-colored glasses firmly in place so as to not burst your bubble of happiness, peek over the rims of those glasses every so often to keep at least one eye on reality.

Just the Facts

Use this stage as an opportunity to explore your potential partner, both inside and out. Ask questions, and really listen to the answers. It is so easy to hear what you want to hear and to overlook what someone is really telling you about him- or herself. Pay attention to what the other person tells you about him- or herself up front. As Oprah Winfrey said in her 1996 speech to the graduation class at Wellesley College, "When people show you who they are, believe them the *first* time."

Ask about the basics. Where does she live? What does she do for a living? What does she do for fun? Does she have any pets? This will give you some insight into her lifestyle and habits.

Ask about his preferences. Does he like music, and what kind? What is his favorite kind of food? What movies does he like? Does he enjoy traveling?

Inquire about her past. Where did she grow up? Where did she go to school? What was her childhood like? Why did she choose her profession? Does she have any brothers or sisters? All this will help you paint a complete picture of who this person is and how she got to be that way.

Watch how he communicates and how he treats people, including waiters, cab drivers, and the ticket taker at the movie theater. Observe him with his friends. All these interactions provide clues into that person's behavior patterns and true nature.

Observe her actions in relation to you. Are they generous? Does she offer you a taste of her meal? Does she interrupt you? Does "thank you" come easily to her? Does she call when she says she will? Noticing little details now will show you how she will behave when bigger issues arise in the future.

Ask about his hopes and dreams. What does he want for himself? What are his goals? What is important to him? This will allow you to go beneath the surface and begin to know who he really is.

At the same time that you are getting to know your potential partner, he is also getting to know you. While you obviously will be inclined to position yourself in the best possible light and be on your best behavior, take care not to mislead the other person into believing you are different from who you really are. By definition, a facade naturally prohibits you from connecting on an authentic level. You will waste both of your time by leading him down a deceptive trail.

Basically, your mission in exploration is to gather information about your potential new partner so that you can later assess whether she is right for you, and vice versa. Take this opportunity to gather as much data as possible; you can never have too much information about someone with whom you are considering a lifelong relationship.

Asking the Hard Questions

It may seem somewhat antithetical to creating a romantic relationship to interrogate your potential partner about where she stands on major life issues. Who wants to talk about religion, personal philosophy, or embarrassing personal concerns when you can gaze into your partner's eyes over a shared dessert? It is a natural instinct to veer away from touchy or delicate subjects that could burst the joy-filled bubble the two of you are in. Instead, you tend to cling to safe topics that will not cause any upset and keep you both in your dreamy state.

Imagine, if instead of getting into a relationship, you were buying a car. You wouldn't just rush into the lot and buy the first flashy car you saw. You would most likely take the time to ask some questions about the car: what kind of gas mileage does it get, how dependable is it, what features are included and which are extra, or how extensive is the service warranty. Perhaps you would research its blue book value, look under the hood, read the odometer, review the service history, and whatever else would ensure you were making a solid purchase. If we put that kind of effort into buying a car, why, then, do so many of us gloss over the important issues when we are procuring a new relationship?

Asking the hard questions early on is the best way to know what you are getting yourself into. Just as checking out a car before buying it can save you the misery of having it break down on the freeway, so, too, will initially discussing the big issues with your partner save you from potential heartbreak later on.

Hard questions can range from how religious he is to whether he has been tested for HIV. One of the delicate issues that people avoid addressing is financial status, as Billy and Leah did. When Leah and Billy got married, they had never really discussed finances. Billy didn't ask, so Leah did not disclose that she had close to $25,000 in debts, including school loans from fifteen years earlier that she was still paying off. When Billy found out about Leah's debt, which was now his debt as well, he felt angry at her for not telling him about it, but he was also unhappy with himself for not approaching the delicate topic of money earlier.

Another delicate issue people might shy away from is whether or not they want to have children. For example, Wendy knew she wanted to have at least two children. When she met Hugh, it seemed presumptuous to her to come right out and ask whether he liked or wanted kids. She didn't want Hugh to think she was trying to rush him into marriage. So she never asked, but simply assumed he would want his own children one day because he often happily relayed endearing stories about his two-year-old niece. When they finally addressed the subject, six months into their relationship, Wendy was surprised to hear Hugh say he did not want to be a father himself, since he did not really want that kind of responsibility. Though Wendy was deeply saddened, she knew she needed to end that relationship before it progressed any further, since the experience of having and raising children was not something she was willing to abandon.

There are ways to ask the hard questions without coming across like an IRS agent. One way is to approach the issue generally, to get a sense of where the person stands. For example, if political affiliation is important to you and you want to know your partner's position, you might bring up the upcoming election or a story you read in the paper about a particular politician. This would invite a conversation about the subject that may give you the insight you are looking for.

Or, if you prefer, you can approach the issue directly, asking gently and without pressure. You can remove the weightiness of the question by asking it in passing, so as not to make the other person feel as though the question is loaded with expectation and consequence. In Wendy's case, she might have said something like "You seem to really enjoy your niece; are you interested in being a father?" If you choose to approach the topic in this manner, take special care with your tone of voice, as that will be what signals your partner that you are asking an important question rather than conducting an inquisition.

In Billy's case, he might have approached Leah before they got married and said something like, "I know this might be awkward, but I figured it was better than both of us guessing what the other person has or does not have. Let's talk about finances." That way, he could have entered their marriage knowing what debts Leah had and avoid feeling deceived.

Granted, asking the hard questions sometimes yields responses that you may not want to hear. No one wants to discover that this wonderful new love has philosophies, life goals, and values directly opposite to hers, or that he has skeletons in his closet. However, at least you will be in possession of all the facts and can make an informed choice about whether this is the right person for you. A veil of unspoken assumptions may protect you from what you don't want to know, but it will also prevent you from discovering the real truths about your potential new partner.

STAGE THREE: EVALUATION

Assuming you and your partner have successfully transited the exploration stage and decided to go forward, you then enter what I call the "make or break" phase: the evaluation stage. Now you have accumulated the information you need and you lay it out before you to assess whether or not you and your partner are truly compatible. You weigh the pros and cons of your relationship and assess whether it is worth your continued investment.

All this may sound somewhat analytical and even harsh, but building a strong union requires that you find your rational mind amidst all the magnificence and wonder of your surging emotions. It is easy to evaluate your partner when you are enraptured—everything he does is wonderful. Yet you will need to look ahead to the future and envision what your relationship will be like when the patina of newness fades and you need to engage in the daily journey of life.

One of the most important things about choosing a love relationship in the first place is choosing it on the correct criteria. I have seen many people over the years choose partners based on something changeable or transitory—looks, money, job, sexual prowess—only to find the relationship collapse the moment one of those features disappears. If a relationship is based upon shared activities and they cease, then what is left? A couple who comes together because of a shared love for skiing must be able to relate when the snow melts in the springtime. If the relationship is based on physical attractiveness and an accident or age changes that, where do they go from there? What happens to a couple whose bond is based on financial freedom if the market crashes? Evaluating your partner on transitory features can be dangerous if they are what lead you to declare them "a match."

Revisiting Your Criteria

If you made criteria lists, now is the time to extract those lists from the drawer and review them to see how close your potential partner comes to what you are looking for. Ideally, that person's essence is exactly what you want, and they possess the majority of the qualities you wrote on your must-have and wish lists and none of the ones on your knockout-punch list. If you have no such lists, you will need to take an objective look at your partner and your relationship and assess what works for you, what doesn't, and what you can and cannot live with. Either way, the process entails observing, evaluating, and choosing whether to continue the relationship or abort it.

If your partner possesses a quality that is on your knockout-punch list or does not possess a quality that is on your must-have list, you will be faced with two choices. One, to abort the relationship, or two, to reevaluate how valid your criterion still is for you.

For example, let's say that one of your original must-have requirements was that the person love to travel, and then the person you meet likes to travel but would just as soon stay home. You will need to either terminate the relationship or reassess how important it is that both of you be passionate about traveling.

You might know in your heart that you cannot give up your

dream of finding someone who is your travel-match, and you then need to set both of you free to find the right mate. If, however, you discover that you are just as happy being with someone who merely *likes* to travel, then you can discard your criterion and proceed with your new relationship.

A note of caution, however: It is tempting to abandon your criteria when you are faced with ending your new relationship. Often we become infatuated with the idea of love or believe that we need the relationship so much that we are willing to ignore our instincts about what will and will not work for us. We convince ourselves that our inner radar is wrong or that the other person will, in fact, change over time. However, the truer you are to yourself and your requirements, the happier you will be in the long run. A little denial in the present can cause a lot of pain in the future.

Denying Your Truth

Annabel, 53, was a professor of literature at a large university. She thrived on reading and the exchange of intellectual ideas, and her criteria for a mate dictated that anyone without a certain level of intelligence was not a match for her. When she met Carl, a younger man with only a junior high school education to whom she was deeply attracted on all levels except an intellectual one, she was presented with a dilemma.

On one hand, Annabel wanted the relationship with Carl to work. He made her laugh and added a needed degree of levity to her life. Plus, she was secretly feeling old and concerned that her time to find a mate was running out. On the other hand, she grew frustrated every time she tried to bring up a conversation about an article she had read or a lecture she had attended, since Carl was ill-equipped or unwilling to respond in a way that stimulated any in-depth conversation. While he was by no means unintelligent, Carl did not feel the same draw to a life of intellectual pursuit as Annabel.

Annabel reassessed how valid her must-have list still was and, against her better judgment, convinced herself that she could sacrifice her need to be mentally stimulated by her partner. She swallowed her feelings and resolved to simply work around whatever Carl could or would not contribute.

Not surprisingly, Annabel's plan did not work. As she discovered, a must have is a difficult criterion to release. As time went on, Annabel's attraction to Carl began to fade, since it lacked the mental spark she needed to keep it aflame. Though it caused her great pain, she eventually admitted that Carl and she were not a match.

Trusting Your Instincts

Evaluating becomes a bit more difficult when the person falls into the gray area of possessing some but not all of the qualities on your wish list. For example, Brooke, who was a freelance nature photographer and an adventurous spirit, wrote on her wish list that she wanted someone who liked to travel and enjoyed seeking out new and exotic experiences. The man she loved, Phil, met almost all her other criteria except for that one. Phil was a sports fan and liked to stay close to home, watching television. He preferred burgers and fries to exotic foods and didn't really like stretching beyond where he felt comfortable. Brooke loved Phil because he was kind, made her feel special, and shared her value of family, but she was unsure whether she wanted to spend her life with someone who did not want to travel the world with her. She felt stuck and came to see me to gain some clarity.

I explained to Brooke that although each person needs to develop her own barometer to measure what ultimately will or will not work for her, *everyone* needs to listen to his or her instinct. As with any difficult choice you need to make in life, you can gather the information, ask for input from those you trust, and read all the "Is he the one for you?" quizzes you come across in magazines, but ultimately the deciding factor will be your inner radar. You will need to clue in to what your heart and head are telling you and go with whatever message comes through the strongest.

You can encourage these messages to rise to the surface in several different ways. You can make an objective list of the pros and cons of this relationship. This will wrestle your dilemma into a more manageable shape and size, rather than allowing it to remain as an enormous and unsolvable maze in your head.

You can call up a vision in your mind of what your life would be like one, five, ten, or fifty years from now if you remained in this relationship. What do you see? Do you like what you see? How does this vision make you feel? The answers will coax your instinctive responses to the surface of your conscious mind.

You can ask yourself the hard questions. Is this the person you want to grow old with? Does he or she have enough of what you want and need for you to take the risk? Are you making a choice based on what you want or what you think you should want? Are you selling out your dream, or are you making a mature choice about what is right for you? Are you trying to stifle your inner truth for the sake of security?

Evaluation is a process that has no right answers. The objective is to create as much certainty as possible in your head, your heart, and your gut in order to be confident and comfortable with whatever you choose. When you can make your choice you will feel confident that you made it knowing that you weighed the options and chose from that centered place within you that knows what is right for you.

STAGE FOUR: BUILDING INTIMACY

If your evaluation led you to conclude that yes, this is the relationship you want to pursue, then you and your partner are ready to move into the next stage of creating love: building the bonds of intimacy. This level brings your relationship deeper beneath the surface and begins the formation of "we."

Intimacy is built through a deepening of your initial connection. In essence, intimacy means the degree to which I let you "in-to-me." It is the degree to which each person is emotionally and inter-personally available to the other. Intimacy is allowing yourself to be vulnerable and, at the same time, making it safe for your beloved to disclose his or her inner reality. It is one of the sweetest parts of re-lating: being able to finish each other's sentences, knowing what the other is thinking, having a deep understanding of your partner's inner machinations, feeling on the same wavelength.

If you and your partner achieve true intimacy, you have the capacity to actually sit and be with each other without having to fill every moment with an activity. You can be together in the silences, listening to what isn't said; you can feel the stillness, calm, or electricity between you and share those moments when your two essences connect at a deeper level. Intimacy is the reward that lies at the center of the sacred space created by the connection of two souls.

Before we enter that space, each of us lives in our own separate world. Our worlds are defined by our individual perceptions of reality, which are comprised of our thoughts, feelings, observations, fantasies, and images. In order to connect separate realities, you must know what your partner is experiencing and vice versa. It is necessary for you both to share secret thoughts, feelings, joys, fears, concerns, dreams, sorrows, pains, and pleasures in order to build the bonds of intimacy.

Picture these bonds as fishing lines strung from one person to another. The more lines you string, the stronger the bond. When your partner confesses to you that he dreams of becoming a pilot, a line is strung. When she rushes to call you first to tell you about her big promotion, another line is strung. When he tells you about how angry he is at his brother for not helping to care for their aging parents, yet another line is strung. And so it goes.

When you have established many strong bonds, the strands are actually substantial enough to construct a bridge between your two separate realities. Imagine hundreds or even thousands of strands connecting both people to form this bond. The more bridges you build, the deeper the connection and trust between the two of you, and the closer you bring yourselves to that divine connection called intimacy.

Tools for Building Intimacy

Building intimacy is an action. While connection and emotional chemistry are important in intimacy, you and your partner can also extend your strands to each other, using specific tools and methods.

The primary method of building intimacy is simply opening the door and allowing your partner to truly see the truth of who you are in all of your dimensions. By telling the hard truths about yourself—the ones that you are not necessarily proud of—you offer your partner the opportunity to see your most basic human side. Exposing your fears, concerns, jealousies, or uncomfortable truths from your past extends you to your partner in your most vulnerable state and invites your partner to accept you fully as you are.

Sharing hopes, wishes, and dreams creates bonds between partners. Just like childhood friends who whisper dreams to each other in the dark, partners can share their innermost desires and deepen their trust. Revealing private thoughts invites your partner in to your innermost world and lets him know that he is a welcome confidant. Withholding builds walls, disclosing builds bridges. It's your choice—walls or bridges.

Simply spending time just being together invites intimacy. When you lie quietly with your partner and listen to her heartbeat and the cadence of her breathing, you connect yourselves on a basic energetic and human level. You begin to flow with each other's rhythms, which allows a new rhythm of "we" to emerge.

STAGE FIVE: COMMITMENT

Commitment is the shift from "I think I want this relationship" to "I *know* I want this relationship." It is the moment you move from uncertainty to certainty, from hesitation to action, and from "maybe" to "yes." It occurs when you have gone through the evaluation process enough to feel so strongly about your choice as to back it with conviction.

Simply because you commit does not mean you are no longer afraid, nor does it mean that you are 100 percent certain that what you are about to do is absolutely the right thing. It means that enough of you believes that this is right, while the rest of you is willing to take the risk of being wrong. Commitment means you put all of your proverbial eggs in one basket and *go for it.*

Allie and Dirk had been dating for nearly a year when Dirk went into the hospital for minor but complicated surgery. Up until then, they had been very happy building their intimate bonds and continuing to explore and evaluate each other, and Allie sensed that she was getting close to releasing her hesitation. When she saw Dirk lying in the recovery ward hooked up to machines and tubes, a wave of love rushed over her, and she thought, "I want to take care of him forever." She knew then that she had made that profound shift, and she was awed and overwhelmed by the enormity of her emotions. She had committed to Dirk in her heart.

Of course, both partners have to commit if the relationship is to last. If one person is committed and the other is not, the relationship can sustain such an imbalance for only a short period of time before impatience and resentments creep in. Thankfully, Dirk felt the same way Allie did, and they are now in a joyful and rewarding committed partnership.

Fear of Commitment

Some people shy away from commitment because they are afraid of making a mistake. They may have a history of past mistakes, for which they mentally flog themselves. If they are suffering the pain of "I should never have gotten involved with . . ." or the regret of ". . . that was the biggest mistake of my life," then chances are they will be reticent, reluctant, and resistant to committing again.

Before they can ever commit to another relationship, they must forgive themselves and heal those wounds. This is something each person must do for himself; no one can do this type of healing for another. It is a solo journey. The only thing you as a partner can do is make it safe for him to disclose his fears and wait for him to be ready. If he takes longer than your patience or timetable allows, then you will need to make a choice about whether to stay or move on.

If you are the one who is willing but unable to make the shift from maybe to yes, then it is your own healing journey you must embark upon. You will need to look inside yourself and examine what is standing in your way. What is the fear that is holding you back? Examining that fear will allow you to know the healing work you need to do for yourself.

Some people want a guarantee that they are making the right choice and that this is "it." Lucy is 35 and has broken off several long-term relationships as soon as they reached the commitment stage because she is never 100 percent convinced that her choice of partner will be the right one. She worries about becoming trapped by a wrong decision.

Commitment does require some measure of risk. There are no guarantees in life, and so the best you can do is search your heart for your truth, and if it tells you that this person is who you want, then you will have to take a leap of faith. You may never be totally 100 percent certain that you are doing the right thing, but at the very least, you will learn some valuable life lessons. At the very most, you will initiate yourself in love's higher realms and experience the bliss of a sacred union.

DESIGNING YOUR RELATIONSHIP

When you have found a wonderful partner and you have both committed to each other, it may seem like the work is over. Actually, the work has just begun. Although you may have created the emotional union of "we," there is still the work of creating the dynamic of "we." In other words, it is now time to consciously design your relationship.

You have built a solid emotional foundation for your relationship; now comes all the rest of the day-to-day relating that you will spend most of your time engaged in. You will need to establish the understanding between you to ensure the durability and longevity of your union. A connection between your hearts and souls will sustain you, but it is the actual dynamic of how you relate that will determine the quality of your experience together.

One reason why 50 percent of all marriages end in divorce is because the partners have never established understanding and agreement between them other than those they repeated at the altar. People meet, fall in love, discuss dreams and goals, address a few issues, and get married. Later on, they discover what they never knew—their ideas about why they are together and what each person expects from the other. People rarely take the time to establish roles and responsibilities or create agreements about how they will conduct their relationship. Time passes and one or both of the partners wakes up one day to discover that he or she is in a marriage that has no ground rules to anchor and sustain it.

CREATING AGREEMENTS

To design your relationship as you both want it to be, begin by establishing certain agreements about how you will relate and communicate. These agreements will be the glue that holds you two together when discord or circumstances threaten to tear you apart.

There is a natural timing to discussing agreements. If you have the discussion too soon, someone can become scared. If you have the discussion too late, you may have established habits and norms that are difficult to reverse. The optimum point to create agreements is shortly after you both have committed to each other and the relationship.

In some religions, betrothed couples sign a covenant which is an agreement between them of how they will treat each other and how they will conduct their marriage.

There is value in creating a covenant between two people in the early stages of commitment to serve as a blueprint for how to conduct the relationship. Whether a covenant is in writing or is an oral agreement is irrelevant; what is truly important is that you take the time to design your relationship. I encourage couples to write their agreements, since writing things down makes them real and is a good reminder when you forget. Do whatever it takes for the two of you. This blueprint will act as a guide when you get lost amidst life's challenges and will keep you anchored to your process.

While the word *covenant* can be intimidating, since it may conjure up images of agreements carved in stone, do not let that deter you. Creating a covenant is really quite a simple task. Begin by sitting down together and discussing what your shared intention is for your union. Start by addressing a few basic questions, like what is the purpose of your union, what you intend to be to each other, and how you will care for your relationship.

Next you can address the ground rules for how you will relate to each other. You can write this as a list of conscious vows you make to each other, as in "we agree to . . ." For example, "We agree to listen to each other's truth, honor it with open ears, take care of each other when we are sick, tell each other when something bothers us," and so on. Or you can simply take a few minutes to make these promises to each other out loud.

You can also include some ground rules for how you will communicate with each other, especially when disagreements arise. For example, no interrupting each other, walking out when angry, making attacking suggestions, insulting, yelling, or physically abusing. This will make disagreements far less unpleasant in the future.

Lastly, discuss how to handle the ups and downs that life may bring. How will you cope together when something tragic or traumatic happens? How do you plan to face adversity? How will you celebrate accomplishments and joyful events? Life can be a roller coaster, and these agreements will act as your safety belt.

If you decide to put your agreements in writing, when you have included everything you want to address, you both should sign the document and put it away in a safe place. You might want to review and revise it each year as needed, as a way to remind yourselves of your understanding and to keep aligned with the purpose and essence of your union.

ESTABLISHING ROLES AND RESPONSIBILITIES

In every relationship, roles and responsibilities are designated whether or not you consciously assign them. Frequently, both partners simply fall into whatever role they feel comfortable playing and there is little to no need for clarification or discussion. Usually one person feels the burden and resentment of doing it all, or something falls between the cracks because each person thought the other person was taking care of it. If roles and responsibilities are not discussed, they are assumed, which inevitably leads to misunderstandings and problems down the road.

Roles and responsibilities come into play in the mundane details of life and the maintenance of your relationship. They cover issues like who manages the finances, who takes out the garbage, who prepares dinner, who repairs things when they break, who drives on long trips, and who walks the dog. It can also include things like which one of you makes social plans with your friends or plans parties, who arranges vacations, which one generally takes over in crises, who is in charge of romance, or which one of you takes leave from a job to raise the children.

While it may not be romantic to designate roles and responsibilities, it is certainly necessary to keep your relationship running smoothly. At the heart of your relationship is your partnership: the entity created by your combined efforts. This partnership is kept balanced by an even division of input and effort that needs to be established and negotiated fairly. There will be little time or energy left to spend enjoying the wonderful rewards of love if you and your partner expend it all quarreling over who does what.

Designating roles and responsibilities may feel businesslike, but businesses do it for a reason. If no one knew who was responsible for what, chances are the business would fail. So while delegating roles and responsibilities in your relationship may feel a bit contrived, do it anyway; it is necessary to keep your partnership running smoothly.

Creating love is a process that will require your patience, resources, and faculties. When you make the necessary shifts in energy and perspective, you invite love in and give it space to grow. By trusting the process and allowing your love to evolve consciously and naturally, you greatly increase your chances of creating a strong and durable foundation that will weather the test of time.

RELATIONSHIPS PROVIDE
OPPORTUNITIES TO GROW

♥

Your relationship will serve as an unofficial "lifeshop" in which
you will learn about yourself and how you can grow
on your personal path.

An authentic relationship can have a profound effect on your life. It can give you a glimpse into your innermost hidden places, clarify what you want and what you need, illuminate the pathway to your emotional and spiritual depths, and teach you valuable life lessons. The most powerful impact it can have is to help you grow and stretch exponentially as a human being.

The definition of growth is "expansion, increase, or augmentation." Relationships not only add to the quality of our lives, they also add to the quality of our *selves*. They expand our horizons and perspectives, increase our awareness of possibilities, augment our resources, and open opportunities to overcome challenges. The energy created from an authentic union carries us through the growth process so that we can emerge as stronger, better, wiser, and "more real" people.

Your relationship provides many different avenues through which you can grow. Primarily, the presence of a beloved in your life creates new possibilities for you. He or she can open doors you never knew existed and present options you might not have considered when you were on your own. Your relationship will excavate your personal issues that need to be healed, stretch your boundaries, and teach you how to relate on an advanced level. Your beloved becomes your partner in your growth process, as you do in his or hers, leading each other down exciting paths and through life-altering challenges.

GAINING NEW PERSPECTIVES

People have certain features, elements that make them uniquely who they are. These features include their knowledge, individual interests, skills, passion, and life experiences. When two people come together in a union, each one brings these features with him or her. Uniting in a relationship offers both partners the opportunity to share those features, offering them to each other as precious gifts.

When Sarah met Benji, she was not much of an outdoorsy person. She had never had the opportunity to go hiking, fishing, or any other such activity, since no one in her life had those interests. She was more of a city girl, happy knowing that the only trekking she would be doing was to the supermarket in a snowstorm. Benji, on the other hand, had been an Eagle Scout until he was 18 and had gone on many hiking and camping expeditions to satisfy his love of the outdoors. He convinced Sarah to go on a three-day white-water rafting trip with him, sleeping in a tent each night and cooking meals over a campfire. Sarah was hesitant at first, since she had never experienced anything like that, but she trusted Benji, so she agreed.

Sarah had the time of her life. Benji taught her how to pitch a tent, make a fire, tell time according to the position of the sun, and mark her trail so she would know how to find the campsite if she got lost. She took to all of this with ease, and by the end of the three days, she was hooked. Benji "gave" her the outdoors—a passion they now share.

As Sarah told me this story, she realized that her perspectives had been broadened by many of the partners in her life. She recalled Paul, who introduced her to the music of Bob Dylan, and Michael, who taught her all about personal finances, and Christopher, who took her to his family's farm in Ireland and showed her a world she never knew existed, and Abe, the artist who coaxed her to learn pottery, which is now one of her favorite hobbies.

Your loved one has much to teach you. Engaging in a relationship with your partner brings you the added bonus of getting to share his interests and hobbies and to learn from his or her expertise. It doubles the breadth of your experiential pool. In turn, you offer your partner the same opportunities, and together, your perspectives are broadened by leaps and bounds.

STRETCHING YOUR COMFORT ZONE

Being in a relationship, by definition, will cause you to come up against the edges of your personal boundaries. You will be called upon to widen your personal limitations and expand beyond the realm of what is normal for you. Up until the point that you and your beloved formed your union, you were able to operate well within your physical, emotional, mental, and spiritual confines. Sometimes you ventured beyond those parameters as life demanded, but unless you are highly dedicated to an advanced personal growth process, you most likely remained within your comfort zone.

The presence of your significant other changes that, for she arrives in the relationship with needs and desires that may require you to extend beyond that comfort zone. This can surface in the most minor of circumstances, as when Penny, who was essentially a homebody, needed to stretch herself to be with Warren, who was an extrovert and liked to socialize with large groups of friends. Penny relayed a story from the early days of their relationship, when Warren asked her to go with him and his five closest couple friends to a major league baseball game. Penny did not want to go. She was worried that Warren would go off with the other men and she would have nothing to say to the other women. Fortunately, Penny had a very wise therapist who explained to her the concept of stretching beyond one's comfort zone. She went to that game, and to her relief, the other women went out of their way to make her feel comfortable.

The need to stretch beyond one's comfort zone can also show up in more major arenas. Harris, a heart surgeon who believed traditional medicine was the only option, met and fell in love with Judy, an energy healer. Harris needed to be willing to make a stretch beyond his beliefs and listen to Judy speak about alternative medicine in order to make space for his beloved's life's work.

A certain amount of give-and-take is required. You and your partner will need to negotiate who needs to accommodate whom and when. As you and your partner move through the machinations of your relating, you will both need to learn to expand your zone of comfort when necessary for the sake of your union. The stretching may feel somewhat uncomfortable at first, but in the end it hurts no more than ordinary growing pains.

SUPPORTING EACH OTHER

Several years ago, my husband and I took a trip to South Africa. We visited a diamond mine, and as we prepared to board the open elevator that would lower us down 700 meters into the mine, I froze. I looked down and knew that I simply could not go on this trip to the bowels of the earth. It looked terrifying, and I could hardly find enough breath to say, "You go ahead, honey. I'll just stay here."

In that moment I had hit the edge of my comfort zone. I could not push myself to get on the elevator. My husband did one simple thing: he took my hand and said, "I'm here with you. It will be okay; I won't leave your side." I looked into his eyes and allowed his support to push me that extra inch and onto that elevator.

Your partner's support can lead you to new heights (or depths). It can be the pillar that props you up when you feel weak or it can be the wind beneath your wings that allows you to fly. In return, your support can move your partner from "I can't" to "I can" and give him the inspiration to expand into greater levels. This is the essence of what it means to *be there* for each other.

Support has many forms. You can support your partner when she lacks confidence by reminding her of all the things she has accomplished. When Lori was faced with a tough deadline on a freelance design project, she panicked and swore that she couldn't do it. Her partner, Stefan, sat her down and made a list of every project she had pulled off in record time to reestablish her belief in her ability.

Support can show up in the form of steady reassurance. Stefan was going through a difficult time looking for a new job; when he grew discouraged, Lori reminded him again and again of her faith in his ability to manifest the outcome he desired. Stefan was able to borrow Lori's faith to sustain him through the process.

You can also extend support through action. Let's say your partner has a dream of writing a novel. To support him, you could perhaps clear out the extra bedroom for him to use as an office and pick up a few books about writing and publishing. These small acts will silently convey your support of his dream.

As you can see, your relationship can provide both you and your partner with the opportunity to support each other and help each other move beyond your limitations into new and exciting terrain. Support can be a powerful motivator that can assist you both in your personal growth process.

Supporting Versus Controlling

There is, however, a danger in taking support too far, as it then veers into enabling or control. Your aim should be to help facilitate your partner through his situation, not climb inside it with him. If your support turns into pushing, then you end up controlling your partner and denying him the opportunity to do his own work. If his resolving his issue becomes more important to you than it is to him, then you end up enabling, doing his work for him and stifling his individual growth process.

Taking over and doing the growing for your partner does not help either of you. Remember, support means to uphold, not take over. The key to finding that balance is to remain external to each other's personal issues.

Neither person in a relationship arrives perfect. Every individual is on a path of continuous improvement, and one of the main benefits of having a loving partner is the support that she offers as you make your way along your path. Two whole people supporting each other is a powerful combination that can ultimately help you both in your personal growth processes.

ILLUMINATING AND HEALING ISSUES

We all have issues. Even the healthiest and happiest of people have some areas in which they need to grow. Most issues are created in childhood and follow us until we work through them. These issues present themselves in the form of lessons to be learned, lessons that will be repeated until learned.

There is no arena in which your issues surface faster or more intensely than in your relationship. Because of the intimate nature of authentic unions, your relationship acts as a flashlight shining light on hidden patterns and places where you need to heal and grow. Your partner will act as a mirror reflecting those illuminated places back to you. When you bear witness to your issues through your partner's eyes and within the context of your relationship, you are given the opportunity to heal them.

I always find it truly amazing how we draw to us the person who embodies the exact issues we need to address. Clara, who had a fear of abandonment, repeatedly drew to her partners who would suddenly withdraw and disappear. John, who had trouble standing up for himself, became involved with Isabelle, who was domineering. Elena married Jose, who possessed similar qualities to her abusive father. This happens because each one of these people unconsciously manifested the person that would enable them to replay the initial source of the issue and offer them the chance to heal it.

Certain basic human issues show up more commonly than others in relationships. In my workshops, I have seen thousands of people work through many different lessons, yet the source of most difficulty in relating stems from a few core issues: fear, control, and boundaries.

FEAR

Fear is the absence of trust. When fear is present, the basis of trust in your relationship is eclipsed, since fear and trust cannot exist in the same space simultaneously. Since trust is such an absolute necessity between partners, it is imperative that you examine and release the fears you have about partnering so that you can connect without hesitation or reservation.

Fears in relationships often arise around the idea of proximity. Relating is about coming close enough to someone to connect while still maintaining enough distance to keep your individual identities. Think about it in terms of your physical space requirements. If someone stands too far away, you will have difficulty hearing him and may feel somewhat separated. Conversely, if he stands too close, you may feel uncomfortable, wishing he would take a step back and allow you your space. Neither scenario is conducive to clear connections.

It is the same with the dance of intimacy. Learning to maintain and be comfortable with the right balance of closeness and distance can be tricky and can cause fear of abandonment or entrapment to arise. The fear of abandonment and its mirror opposite, fear of entrapment, are the most common causes of trust issues in love relationships.

If abandonment is your issue, you may find yourself in relationships that are tenuous, undermined by a silent threat of termination. You wait expectantly for the other shoe to drop and react in one of two ways—clinging, which usually drives your partner away, or you leave first, to avoid the abandonment you perceive as inevitable. Either way, your expectation of being left alone is fulfilled.

Abandonment issues almost always arise from childhood. They can stem from something as simple as crying in your bedroom with no response to the extreme of a primary caretaker actually walking out on you. The belief is "I am not lovable enough for someone to stay"; the lesson that you will need to learn is that you *are* lovable enough for someone to stay. Believing this will alter the expectations you emit and hence change the results you are experiencing. This lesson will resurface in your relationships again and again until you heal the underlying belief that mandates it.

If entrapment is your issue, you will feel suffocated whenever someone gets too close. Entrapment, the inverse of abandonment, is the fear that you will never be given enough space because that other person is overly smothering. Entrapment fears can stem from growing up in a controlling environment or one in which you had no privacy, space, or time alone.

Peter had a severe fear of entrapment. As a child, his mother controlled every aspect of his life, from what he ate to the socks he wore. Subsequently, as an adult, every time he got close to someone, he experienced emotional claustrophobia.

Not surprisingly, Peter drew to him Suzanne. Suzanne was overly controlling and stepped right into Peter's mother's old shoes. Having every detail of his life dictated by Suzanne, from what brand of suits he wore to what magazine he subscribed to, felt very familiar to Peter, but at the same time feelings of panic began to arise in him. As was his usual pattern, Peter let the situation escalate until he could stand it no more and fled.

The lesson in entrapment is to learn to overcome the panic and actually *stay*, even though at times it feels smothering. The key is to trace and pinpoint the origin of the feeling that arises from within you and then to assess what action you need to take.

CONTROL

A control issue stuns the flow of energy between two partners. If either partner is a controlling person, he or she cannot participate in the give-and-take process necessary in an authentic relationship, since he or she will always need to be in command of how things are done. An authentic relationship will require that you both yield to what "we" want as opposed to what each "I" wants, and by being controlling, you prevent the "we" from ever becoming a solid entity.

Mitch had a control issue, though he didn't know it until Hope pointed it out to him. He always needed to be the one who drove, who made the plans, and who determined when and how much time they spent together. Whenever Hope made a suggestion, Mitch would "one up" her and suggest someplace bigger, better, fancier, or more expensive. At first, Hope was flattered that he wanted to be so generous and doting, but eventually she began to feel like the relationship was all about him and not about them. She felt like a marionette controlled by Mitch's strings.

Hope eventually pointed out this dynamic to Mitch, who at first reacted defensively to her "accusation" that he was overly controlling. Yet when she laid out the examples before him, one by one, explaining all the situations that he had taken over or manipulated to his own wishes, Mitch began to see Hope's point. She expressed to him how invalid his actions made her feel, which allowed Mitch to see that his behavior was hurting the woman he loved. He was astonished to see how rigid he had become and agreed to work on this issue within himself, and with her.

Though this continues to be a point of negotiation and sometimes contention between Hope and Mitch, he is using his relationship as an opportunity to learn how to behave in a new and different way. Now, when Hope suggests an activity, Mitch stops himself from trying to alter her suggestion and practices letting go of his need to have everything be done his way all the time. Not long ago, Hope called me to tell me that Mitch agreed to go on a "romantic surprise" weekend that she planned for them entirely without his input.

If control is your issue, you will need to learn to let go of your rigidity. Your love relationship can be an excellent opportunity to practice this, for nowhere is it more essential that you share the driver's seat.

BOUNDARIES

Maintaining boundaries is a big issue for many people. Boundaries establish the outline of who you are and what you are and are not willing to do. When you become involved in a love relationship, these divisions can become blurred. That blurring causes fuzziness about where one person leaves off and the other person begins.

Porous Boundaries

If you have a boundary issue, it may show up as being too porous (i.e., too nice). Joni had a lifelong problem with this. She would verbally encourage people to encroach on her territory, issuing kind invitations to her time and effort. She wanted to be open and accommodating, but she usually ended up overextending herself and feeling resentful. When she said things like "By all means call me whenever you need me," she was secretly thinking, "I'm so tired; I wish everyone would stop calling me and asking me to do things for them." She would extend herself out of her natural spirit of generosity, but then become overwhelmed and annoyed when people took advantage of her offers.

When Joni met Stuart, she immediately fell into her automatic routine of overextending herself. She agreed to see Stuart whenever he suggested, and often canceled her preexisting plans to accommodate him. She offered to do sweet things like pick up his cat from the vet if he was too busy at work or find a tie to go with his hunter-green suit. When Stuart needed to write a long proposal for his job, Joni offered to lend her writing skills to the project and ended up doing a large percentage of the work. She adored Stuart and was initially happy to give as much of herself as she could to make him happy.

After a while, Stuart got used to this kind of attention and he grew to expect it from Joni. But as the months went on, Joni began to feel overwhelmed by the demands placed on her. Her own needs were eclipsed by Stuart's, and she never had any time of her own. Joni began to feel frustrated and resentful, and she once again found herself feeling taken advantage of in a situation created by her own hand.

Joni's lesson was to know her limits. She needed to learn just how much she was willing to offer to someone so she could stop the cycle of overgiving and the resulting overwhelmed feeling and resentment. Though her generous offers usually arose from her kind spirit, she needed to recognize when she was crossing her own boundary and keep herself in check.

Standing Up for Yourself

A boundary issue may show up in having difficulty standing up for yourself or your choices. Take, for example, Fiona. When Josh asked what she wanted to do for her birthday, she told him the truth: what she most wanted to do was spend the evening alone with him at a romantic restaurant. Her idea of the perfect evening was a candlelit dinner for two, and she was delighted when he made a reservation at an expensive restaurant in town that would provide just the atmosphere she wanted. When the day of her birthday arrived, a group of their friends surprised them at their front door and insisted on taking Fiona and Josh out to celebrate her special day.

Josh was delighted at the gesture and turned to Fiona enthusiastically. "I think it will be fun," he said excitedly. "Of course, it's your birthday, and the choice is up to you."

Fiona was crestfallen. She had had her heart set on spending this momentous evening alone with Josh, and she now felt pressure to alter her plans and go out with them. Though she smiled pleasantly, Fiona was crying on the inside. The last thing she wanted to do was cancel their plans to join this big, noisy group, but she felt unable to say so. Their insistence grew more persistent, and Fiona finally reluctantly gave in rather than taking Josh aside and reinforcing what she really wanted. She spent her entire birthday dinner silently beating herself up for not holding firm to her original choice.

When they arrived back home later that night, Fiona stomped around the house like a child preparing for a tantrum. Josh asked what was wrong, which unleashed a torrent of accusations about how he never took her feelings into account, how miserable she'd been at dinner, and how he hadn't even noticed. She told him how much she resented his ruining her entire birthday by being so insensitive to her wishes. Both Fiona and Josh went to sleep feeling like they missed a moment that mattered.

It took Fiona quite a few weeks to forgive herself for not being stronger and standing up for what she truly wanted. She eventually apologized to Josh, admitting that she knew that he could not be expected to read her mind and that it was not his responsibility to stand up for her wishes if she did not do it herself. She promised both Josh and herself that to the best of her ability she would not repeat that dynamic. Since that evening, standing up for herself and her choices has not been a problem.

LEARNING LIFE LESSONS

Your relationship is an unofficial "lifeshop," which teaches you how to relate while you are actually in the process of relating. A lifeshop is a 24-hour-a-day, intensive program of interpersonal skills. You learn as you go and by experimenting with different methods until you find what works. The skills you learn in the context of your relationship award you an advanced degree in relating, which will prove helpful in your interactions with the rest of the world.

The opportunity to learn these skills is presented in the form of life lessons. There are basic lessons that we are all presented with at one time or another if we engage in love relationships. Among them are sharing, patience, gratitude, acceptance, and forgiveness. Throughout the course of your relationship, situations will arise that will demand you learn these lessons (and relearn them as needed).

SHARING

You will need to learn the valuable lesson of sharing within the context of your relationship. Without sharing, a partnership is merely a grouping of two individuals looking out only for themselves. Sharing is the essence of teamwork and partnership. Each person will need to learn it and reremember it whenever the urge to withhold arises to ensure that the dynamic of "we" is maintained.

In relationships, sharing extends to your body, emotions,

thoughts, time, space, and personal belongings. Take Miriam, for example. Long before she met Lloyd, Miriam had mastered self-sufficiency. She earned well over six figures, purchased her home, car, and most of the material possessions she wanted. Miriam had no difficulty with boundaries. Her issue was sharing her life and possessions with her mate, Lloyd.

Lloyd had a good heart. He was nurturing and caring, and could not do enough for Miriam. He was surprised when he discovered Miriam's ideas that what was hers was hers alone, and that she had no intention of sharing with him. She would not allow him to drive her car or use her computer, and she said no when Lloyd asked her if he could stay at her house while she was away on a business trip because his home was being repainted. Whenever Lloyd offered to help her with anything, from moving heavy objects to figuring out directions, she would insist she could handle it on her own. She refused to share her thoughts or worries about her business with Lloyd, saying that it was not his concern. The more rigid Miriam became, the more she shut Lloyd out of their "we-ness."

One day, after Miriam refused to allow Lloyd to use her favorite coffee mug, he asked her if she really wanted to be in a relationship with him. "Of course I do" was her immediate response. "I love you."

"Then let me in," Lloyd responded just as passionately. "Let me share your life—your thoughts—your feelings—your coffee mug! Stop treating me like an outsider."

Lloyd's words opened Miriam's eyes to her behavior. She began to see how she had been treating Lloyd and realized that she needed to open up her life to the man she loved. She needed to begin by believing that Lloyd would not take advantage of her. She realized that by sharing her life and her possessions, she would be offering far more to her beloved than car keys and coffee mugs. She would be offering her trust. It wasn't easy, but Miriam retrained herself and learned how to share.

PATIENCE

Patience is a virtue not only in life but in love as well. Every person moves, grows, and evolves according to his or her own individual pace and rhythm. In partnerships, each person needs to learn to respect the other's timetable, be it in the physical, emotional, intellectual, or spiritual realm.

Gina wanted to get engaged to Evan. She felt she—and they—were ready. Evan, on the other hand, though he loved Gina very much and was deeply committed to her, was not quite ready for such a step. When Gina grew frustrated, Evan assured her from his heart that he did want to marry her one day, but that he was just not ready to be a husband. Gina knew she wanted to spend the rest of her life with Evan, so she needed to learn the lesson of patience in the short term. Gina believed that Evan's feelings and intentions were sincere, so she was able to contain her frustration and wait for Evan to be ready to walk down the aisle.

Celia needed to learn a different version of patience. She had always been a fast-paced individual who liked to get things done quickly. She walked briskly, ate her food rapidly, and usually drove well over the speed limit. Then, since opposites often manage to attract each other, Celia met and fell in love with Paul, who generally moved at a slower pace. Paul liked to stroll and savor his food, and he usually drove a few miles per hour under the speed limit.

Celia was often impatient with Paul, drumming her fingers on the table while waiting for him to finish his food and sighing audibly whenever another car whizzed past them on the highway. One day, as Celia was literally pulling Paul by the hand to make him walk faster, Paul stopped in his tracks and said, "Why are we always in such a rush? I feel like we're in a race to get through life, when what I really want to do is slow down and enjoy every moment with you!"

It worked. Celia realized that she needed to stop trying to force her own pace on to her partner. She still moves like lightning when she is by herself, but when she is with Paul, she tries to slow down a little and just enjoy being together.

GRATITUDE

Your relationship will require that you learn the lesson of gratitude, to ensure that you never take your loved one for granted. Learning to appreciate your partner for all that he or she is and all that he or she does is what enables you to reinforce your connection to him or her each and every day.

Cammy and Doug had been married for 15 years. They had a traditional marriage in that he was the provider and she was the nurturer and caretaker. Life had dealt them their fair share of ups and downs, including a lawsuit that forced Doug to change careers in midlife. Starting over was hard on everyone, especially because it meant a serious cut in pay.

Doug told Cammy that the best thing they could do was get into real estate and use their skills to renovate and sell homes. The real estate market was on the upswing, and they were in a financial position to buy, renovate, and then sell; it was the ideal new venture they could do with virtually no past experience. Cammy agreed. For one year, they bought house after house, cleaned, painted, carpeted, tiled, and financed them, then sold them for a profit. It was hard work, and they both struggled to do their parts.

One day, after they had been scraping paint for hours, Doug looked at Cammy with her bandana on her head, smudges of dirt on her cheeks, and sweat on her brow, and was overcome with gratitude. He had always appreciated Cammy's loyalty, but suddenly he realized that perhaps she didn't know it. He walked over to her, took her hand, and said, "You are the one; I wouldn't want to go through this with anyone else. We may not be rich, but we're happy and we're together, and I'm so lucky to be with you."

Cammy was startled at first, but she quickly realized that Doug was simply saying "thank you" for hanging in there. It only took a moment for him to say those words, but she felt the impact of Doug's words deep inside for many years. As Doug and Cammy learned, a little gratitude goes a long way in love relationships.

ACCEPTANCE

Acceptance is one of those lessons that you will need to learn and practice every day within the context of your relationship. It extends from acceptance of your partner's quirks and perceived flaws to acceptance of the way he does things. As you will learn in Rule Six, every couple has to deal with differences. The groundwork for dealing with those differences begins with a basic willingness to accept your partner *exactly as he is.*

How can you accept those things that irritate, annoy, or even anger you? The answer is, by extending to your partner the same unconditional understanding and acceptance that you wish for yourself and learning to live with those characteristics that grate on you. While your partner might bring you joy, she was not placed on Earth only to please and accommodate you. She exists as an entity unto herself, and while making you happy is ideally a goal of hers, it is not the *only* goal. Remembering that she is human with needs, wants, and agendas, just like you, will help immeasurably in learning the lesson of acceptance.

Terry loved anything technological, whereas his wife, Sheila, was a technophobe. Sheila would rather make lists on paper than use a computer—a preference that was completely alien to Terry. To him, computers were awe-inspiring machines, and he could not comprehend Sheila's reluctance to learn how to use one. He spent many hours listing the benefits of transferring her systems onto computer disks rather than into her daily planner and checkbook.

After months of listening to Terry try to convince her of the merits and wonders of a laptop, Sheila felt she needed to address the situation. She explained to Terry that she was simply not drawn to computers, and just as she would not try to convince him to *not* use one, she would appreciate it if he would respect her choice to keep her systems the way they were. She asked him to please accept her position, whether he understood it or not.

Terry complied, though he was still baffled as to why anyone would not embrace technology. He loved that Sheila accepted all his quirks, including his habit of ordering too many unnecessary components for his hardware, and he could see the fairness of offering the same unconditional acceptance of her point of view.

Do you accept your partner as he or she is? If you don't, try to imagine how it would feel if your partner did not accept something about you. Perhaps that will help you see how one of the most precious gifts love can offer is unconditional acceptance.

FORGIVENESS

Nowhere is forgiveness of transgressions more loaded than in love relationships. When two people form a union that is supposed to be based on trust and that trust is violated, it takes great strength and strides to forgive. However, since everyone has lessons to learn, including your partner, forgiveness is sometimes required. Your relationship will offer you many opportunities to learn the lesson of forgiveness.

Each time you are faced with words or circumstances that violate your basic agreements, you will have a choice—to hold on to your anger or to shift into forgiveness. Anger makes you smaller, while forgiveness forces you to grow beyond what you were. Choosing forgiveness is not easy, but it is the only option if you are committed to staying in your relationship and keeping it authentic.

For example, Bert and April had just bought a new car. They had saved for close to a year to buy the car they wanted, and they were both delighted with their purchase. One day, April was driving the car alone and looked into the rearview mirror to put on lipstick. As she did, she took her eyes off the road and hit another car. Luckily, she was not going fast enough for anyone to be injured, but both cars sustained considerable damage. It took Bert a few days to forgive April for being careless, but he knew that holding on to his anger was only adding anguish to his wife's guilt, so he released it and they put the drama of the incident behind them.

Unfortunately, at times you may need to forgive more major,

significant transgressions, such as a withheld communication, a mistruth, or a violation of part of your basic agreement. These are the times that are the darkest and most challenging, since you will need to comb the depths of your heart to find the strength and willingness to forgive.

Forgiving your mate does not mean that you condone his or her actions, nor does it mean you roll over and merely accept when you have been wronged. Rather, it means that you feel and work through all your feelings, and then eventually find your way back to seeing your partner as someone who is human, just like you. This is one of the most difficult lessons to learn, but as you will learn in Rule Nine, you must master it if your relationship is to last.

If you allow your relationship to carry you on its course of wonder and discovery, you will see your world opened to remarkable new insights and occasions for growth. The true purpose of an authentic relationship is to bring joy, pleasure, and opportunities for growth. Seizing these opportunities allows both people to learn about themselves—their capacities, their limits, the areas they need to heal, and the specific lessons that will enrich their own life path.

Rule Five

COMMUNICATION IS ESERNTIAL

♥

*The open exchange of thoughts and feelings is
the lifeblood of your relationship.*

*C*ommunication is the main tool partners use to connect with each other. It is the way they extend themselves to each other, letting the other person know who they are, what they need and desire, and how they feel. It is the way in which they inform, educate, support, and negotiate. At its essence, communication is the most vital energy that keeps relationships alive and flowing.

Real communication is more than just speaking and listening, though those elements are certainly required; it is about creating open passageways for information about thoughts and feelings to flow without hesitation or fear of backlash. It is based on mutual respect and understanding, and a willingness to expose your truths, no matter how intense they may be, and allowing your partner to do the same. This kind of exchange is essential if you seek to create an authentic and lasting union, for without good communication, a relationship is merely a hollow vessel carrying you along on a frustrating journey fraught with the perils of confusion, projection, and misunderstanding.

Communication acts as the medium through which you build bridges to your partner. Each person comes to a relationship with his or her own perception of reality, and it is only through communication that two people can connect those two realities. By building those bridges, partners begin to create a hallowed space between them that will serve as the foundation of every interaction they have with each other and lead them toward greater and deeper intimacy.

Lili and Charles met at a cocktail party on a rooftop. They were introduced by a mutual friend, and as they talked, the topic of why men and women cannot seem to understand each other became the topic of a good-natured but somewhat heated debate. Charles said it was because women never admitted what they really wanted, thus making men guess—usually incorrectly. Lili countered that women *do* say what they want, but men simply do not listen carefully enough to hear it. They both laughed and agreed that if men and women would just alter their style of communicating, love would stand a far greater chance of survival. It is now nine months later, and Lili and Charles are very happy together, having made open and clear communication the number one priority in their relationship.

The secret to Lili and Charles's success in relating stems from the fact that they both understand how essential clear communication is. If their lines of communication are open and unfettered, then the possibility is created for them to be aligned with each other's wants, needs, longings, fears, and views, thus allowing them to build strong, intimate bonds.

Without clear communication, there is no means through which partners can bridge their inner realities. They remain two single people engaged in a paired dynamic, which looks like a partnership from the outside but lacks the invisible webbing that connects their hearts and souls. They may experience feelings of isolation and loneliness despite the presence of their partner in their life, for nothing creates a more poignant ache than being in close proximity yet emotionally distant.

THE ART OF COMMUNICATING EFFECTIVELY

Communication is a skill that must be learned like any other. Most of us are fortunate enough to be born with the basic capacity to speak and hear, but to learn the advanced art of communicating requires much more. It demands that you are clear about your own thoughts and feelings, that you are willing to tell the truth about them, that you have the skill to express them effectively and that you have the capacity to listen to your partner's truth without defensiveness or judgment.

There are ten basic steps you can follow to communicate effectively. These steps will enable you to get your message across clearly, whether requesting something trivial or monumental from your partner, expressing anger or minor irritation, or pronouncing an emotion or simple pleasure. The intensity of the message is irrelevant, since these steps apply to any exchange of information you wish to make.

THE TEN STEPS:

1. *Know what you want to communicate.* Sort out what exactly you want to say to someone, so that you do not get stuck in the nonwords ("um," "hmm," "uh," "well") and dilute your message.

2. *Know what outcome you want from the conversation.* You need to know if your aim is to deliver information, get information, explore options, or create action. Knowing the purpose and desired outcome of the communication will keep you aligned with your message.

3. *Choose the right time and place.* So often, people rush to deliver their message without first asking if the other person is in the frame of mind to hear it. Be sure to approach your partner when he or she has the time and the capacity to listen and ensure that the environment is appropriate. You do not want to communicate a message of significant emotional impact while your partner is engrossed in the World Series.

4. *Release the emotion surrounding the message.* This will allow you to be more in control of what you want to say. Find some way to release the charge (vent to a friend, write it out, exercise, go to a recycling center and smash glass, etc.) so that you can allow the recipient to focus on the *content* of what you are saying rather than your emotion.

5. *Set the stage.* Lay your groundwork. Let the recipient know that the purpose of your communication is to put him or her in the right frame of mind. If appropriate, share your feelings about addressing this particular communication. For example, "I feel uncomfortable addressing this, however, I need to ask you something . . ."

6. *Speak from your feelings (rather than judgments).* This will keep you focused on your truth and still allow you to communicate with love. Messages delivered with sincerity generally command more attention and respect.

7. *Deliver your message in syntax and language that the recipient can*

understand. Present your reality in a manner that makes sense to the other person, one he or she can relate to. If you are delivering information or expressing a thought, present it as a statement. If you require input or information, pose it as a question. Confusing the two blurs the issue and puzzles the recipient as to what is expected of him or her.

8. *Ask for confirmation, clarification, and feedback.* This will open the dialogue between you and your recipient and show you that your message was clearly delivered.

9. *Switch roles as necessary.* After you ask for feedback, you need to then move from "communicator" to "recipient" so that the other person can communicate his or her reality to you.

10. *Obtain closure.* Acknowledge the agreed-upon outcome and solidify how it will be deployed by each person.

HOW COMMUNICATION BREAKS DOWN

Communication can break down in an instant. All it takes is one unconscious moment, crossed signal, or unexpressed assumption for the spiral of attack and defend to begin and the transmission lines to shut down. The key to preventing such breakdowns is to be aware of the potential triggers and to take care to circumvent them.

CROSSED SIGNALS

All too often communication breaks down because of misunderstandings or unclear messages. Recently, my friend Wendy asked her husband, Jack, to pick her up the following day at the airport at 6:00. She arrived at the terminal and waited outside until 6:45, but Jack never showed up. She went to the phone and called him, surprised when she woke him up.

"What are you doing there?" she asked. "You're supposed to be at the airport picking me up!"

Jack was just as surprised to hear from Wendy, since he hadn't expected her until 6:00 P.M., and it was only 6:45 A.M. Since she had never specified that she would be arriving on an early morning flight, he figured that meant she would be arriving at the more human hour of 6:00 P.M. Wendy took a cab home and promised herself and Jack she would be more specific the next time.

Communication can also become clouded when it is exchanged through the filter of one or both person's preoccupations or issues. One of my favorite stories that illustrates this is of Ed and Eileen, a couple who have been married for more than 30 years. Ed was soaking in the tub early one evening to relieve his aching muscles, which were bothering him after a long day on the golf course. He was focused on the blisters on his feet when Eileen came home sometime around 6 o'clock.

The whole way home from her afternoon bridge game, Eileen had been worried about whether or not Ed remembered to feed their dog, Buffy. She was focused on Buffy's evening meal when she knocked on the bathroom door and called to Ed in a concerned tone, "Did you feed her?"

Ed, still focused on his feet, thought Eileen was being solicitous and had asked him, "Do your feet hurt?" so he replied, "Just the little toes." Eileen was still so focused on Buffy that she mistakenly thought Ed had replied, "No, just a little *toast.*"

"*Toast?*" she said incredulously. "Why would you feed the dog toast?"

Needless to say, when Ed got out of the tub, they finally figured out how far the miscommunication had gone and shared a good laugh. This story shows how easy it is for the perception of exchanged information to be colored by each person's individual perspective. This particular breakdown happens to be amusing, but it shows how easy it is for lines to get crossed and misunderstandings to arise. You might imagine how complicated things can become when big issues surface, and how such situations can cause real problems if they had missed links on something more consequential.

When signals become crossed and links are missed, it is easy to let the situation go and chalk it up to a "misunderstanding." If you don't clear it up, however, then there is nothing to prevent the situation from reoccurring. To clear it up, both partners will need to figure out what went wrong, take responsibility for their part, forgive the other person for what he or she did, and find ways to prevent the situation from repeating itself in the future. Jack and Wendy now make sure to specify morning or evening when making arrangements, and Ed and Eileen laughingly agreed that perhaps communicating through the bathroom door with the water running is not necessarily optimum conditions.

BENDING THE TRUTH

A bent, withheld, or broken truth is one of the surest ways to erode communication and trust. If one person is caught in a mistruth, then mistrust arises and a wall is built between the partners. Even if the mistruth is not revealed, unspoken barricades are erected out of the energy created by withheld secrets. Either way, there is a glitch in the communication flow that leads to division rather than union.

The essence of true communication is disclosure. With each exchange, partners have a choice to draw closer to each other by disclosing their truths or to move further apart by keeping secrets, refusing to share what is inside them. As I said in chapter three, withholding builds walls while disclosing builds bridges. It's your choice—walls or bridges.

Often you can build walls without even being aware that you are doing so, as in Blaire's case. Blaire liked to buy clothes and often went over the agreed budget. Whenever that happened, Blaire would sneak her packages into their apartment when Jeffrey wasn't looking, immediately remove the tags from her new purchases, and hide them away in the closet as if they had always been there. If

Jeffrey noticed one of her new items and asked about it, she would innocently say, "This? I've had it for years."

What Blaire didn't realize was that the energy she used concealing and protecting her secret was energy that was constructing a wall between Jeffrey and her. The part of her that was responsible for maintaining the secret was the part that was unavailable to Jeffrey and therefore unavailable for any bridge building.

Whether you bend the truth about something minor, like clothing purchases, or major, like an infidelity, the outcome is similar. A wall is built, communication is compromised, and opportunities to connect are lost. Remember, you can build walls or bridges, but not both.

PROJECTED ASSUMPTIONS AND EXPECTATIONS

We all enter relationships with certain expectations of how things should be. We bring with us our assumptions about how relationships should feel and how our partner should behave, speak, dress, drive, eat, order wine, brush their teeth, do laundry, set the table, and make love, all according to what we perceive as correct. For most of us, it is not that we expect our partner to be "perfect," but rather that we would like them to do things exactly as we would expect them to.

As we grow up, we are imprinted with a certain perspective. We learn from our caretakers, both directly and indirectly, what "normal" is, and with that image etched in our minds, we set out into the world expecting it to conform to our reality. Often we are unconsciously playing out the same patterns our parents played out—both the effective and the ineffective ones—because these patterns are so deeply ingrained in us. These patterns exist as a filter of how things "should be."

Because every person comes from a family of origin that is unique, we all have assumptions about "normal" that are equally as disparate. When two people's sets of assumptions collide, there is an eruption. Frustration abounds as these two people grow more and more agitated, unconsciously trying to make the other person conform to what each perceives as the "right" way to be. This is where the vicious cycle of misunderstanding, disappointment, accusation, and wall building begins.

As you can see, assumptions can wreak havoc on relationships. They cause us to project unspoken expectations onto our partners and set them up to disappoint us. Your partner is not a mind reader, and no matter how close you are, she can never really know exactly what is going on in your mind and what you are feeling at every moment. It is up to you to tell her what you are feeling, what you want her to know, and to ask for what it is that you want from her.

Assumptions also rob you of the communication process. If you assume you know what the other person wants, chances are you won't ask. You will miss out on the opportunity to have the essential exploratory conversations that weave together the inter-personal fibers between two people. Assumptions gloss over the inquiry process and stifle the spirit of disclosure.

In almost every relationship I have facilitated over the years, assumptions, conjectures, and expectations are a source of misunderstanding. In fact, whenever a conflict between partners arises, it is almost always because of unconscious assumptions and conjectures and the resulting unexpressed expectations. Here are just a few examples; see if you recognize anyone you know.

Darren wanted to take Holly on a special date to celebrate their six-month anniversary. He made reservations at a popular, expensive restaurant, assuming Holly would love it. In his mind, who wouldn't love an extravagant dinner at the most "in" place in town? When he told Holly where they were going, she was disappointed, since she assumed Darren would want to go to a quiet, intimate, and romantic restaurant, just as she did.

Samantha was a romantic. She believed that if a man cared about a woman, he expressed it lavishly with flowers, love poems, and frequent surprise gifts. Mark was more of a realist, and his way of expressing love was through practical measures such as sending her the edition of *Consumer's Digest* containing information about fax machines, which he knew she wanted, or giving her a new pair of boots for Valentine's Day to keep her feet warm in the winter. Samantha was always disappointed, since Mark did not fit her image of the romantic prince, and Mark was always frustrated, since he could never figure out what he was doing wrong.

Brian grew up with a mother who dedicated her entire life to raising his brothers and him. When he married Jessie, he simply assumed she would do the same for their children. Jessie, however, loved her career as a newspaper editor, and though she certainly planned to have children, she did not plan to abandon her career and stay home full-time to take care of them. Though she knew plenty of women who did this and respected their choices, Jessie knew this would not be right for her. Brian and Jessie hit an impasse: she was angry with Brian for foisting his expectation on to her and Brian was angry with her for not complying with his image of how a wife "should" be.

The Way Out of the Assumption Maze

The antidote to assumptions consists of three parts: awareness, examination, and communication. To become aware of your assumptions, you need to recognize when there is a gap between your expectation and the reality of the situation, then excavate the assumption underneath that expectation. Let's look at Samantha, who was disappointed when Mark did not send her flowers for Valentine's Day. Read closely as I explain how I walked her through the process:

> *What are you feeling?*
> SAMANTHA: Let down.
> *Why?*
> SAMANTHA: I didn't get flowers.

What does receiving flowers mean to you?
SAMANTHA: That I am loved.
Does Mark know that?
SAMANTHA: Well, no, but he should.

Upon excavating her assumption that Mark should know what she wants, and the belief underneath it that flowers equal love, Samantha became aware of her unspoken expectation that Mark would send her flowers for Valentine's Day. She expected Mark to simply behave according to her expectations by either possessing the same standards himself or being able to read her mind to find out hers.

With the assumption excavated and laid out before you, you can then examine whether the assumption is still valid and true for you. If it is not, you can discard it and the expectation that arises from it. If it is still valid for you, then you will need to communicate it to your partner so that he or she can become aware of it and the two of you can negotiate an outcome that works for both of you. In Samantha's case, she realized that although flowers gave her joy, the absence of them did not necessarily bring sadness or signify that someone did not love her. She discarded her assumption that flowers equaled love.

However, after examining her beliefs and preconceived notions, Samantha could have just as easily concluded that flowers are, in fact, necessary to make her feel loved. In that case, she would need to communicate that expectation to Mark so that he could then make an informed choice about how to handle the next Valentine's Day.

THE NEED FOR A SAFE ENVIRONMENT

You can possess the best communication skills in the world, yet these skills will be of no use to you if you are afraid to use them. The challenge of communicating clearly and honestly is made all the more difficult if you are faced with the fear of rejection, criticism, or any other form of hostility. In order for communication to be optimum, a safe environment needs to be created so that both partners feel comfortable expressing their honest thoughts and feelings.

Being "safe" means that you can fully be who you are. You feel encouraged to express all of you, and you are willing to take risks, expose your inner realities, and be vulnerable, for you know that no one will hurt you. You feel fully accepted and therefore have the courage to reveal your deepest truths.

SUSPENDING JUDGMENT

For an environment to truly be safe, there must be a suspension of judgment from both sides. Judgments and criticisms create a climate that feels constricted, stressful, and threatening, and force many people to fold inwardly rather than risk discomfort or pain by putting themselves on the line. A safe and supportive environment opens the lines of communication and deepens the intimacy between the partners, while a threatening environment shuts down communication and creates a gap between them.

In order to make the environment safe for your beloved, you must withhold judgment: listen to your mate's thoughts and feelings, hear her perceptions, concerns, or worries *without commenting, criticizing, or attacking.* You must suspend judgment of her words and actions and allow her to express herself in the safety of your presence, without fear of disapproval or rejection. You will need to allow your partner to say whatever is on her mind in a "blue sky" environment of unconditional support, encouragement, and acceptance.

For example, if your partner tells you that he has reached his tolerance level with his job and he plans to quit, a suspension of judgment might require you to listen without immediately demanding to know how he plans to continue earning money or suggesting he is acting in haste. If your beloved confesses that he does not want to visit your parents because he feels unwelcome, you might need to suspend judgment and encourage your partner to tell you more about these feelings rather than invalidating them.

Suspending judgment of your partner can be easier if you imagine that you are listening to a child who is afraid to tell the truth. When my daughter Jennifer came to me as a child with a certain look on her face, I always encouraged her to tell me the truth by assuring her she would not be reprimanded for it. When you listen to your partner with gentleness and compassion, you can set aside the part of you that is searching for a flaw to pounce upon. That kind of acceptance keeps you aligned as partners rather than shifting to being opponents, and enables you both to feel safe to show each other all of who you are.

REACTING WITHOUT DEFENSIVENESS

It is human nature to defend when we feel we are being attacked; that mechanism was built into our molecular programming thousands of years ago to ensure our survival in the wild. Unfortunately, however, that mechanism kicks in regardless of whether you are being stalked by a predator or criticized by your mate for leaving your socks on the floor. Though relationships are challenging at times, they do not require the same level of aggressive survival skills as in the wild, so you will need to learn how to adjust any defensive reactions accordingly.

It is particularly difficult to suspend judgment when your partner discloses information that is hurtful or offends you. Yet, if you encourage your partner to tell her truth, you must in turn be willing to hear it. If you hear something that feels like it is being aimed at or against you, your reaction will naturally be to defend yourself; the moment that you draw your shield is the moment that the environment ceases to be safe for either of you.

Most disagreements that arise between partners get pulled into a cycle of attack, defend, retaliate, and so on until one is wounded, both are exhausted, or one gives up. The only way out of this cycle is for both people to change it by listening to what the other person has to say without reacting defensively and retaliating. It takes one of you moving out of "fight" and "right" mode for the exchange to lose its heat and return the environment to one that is emotionally safe for both of you.

Listening without defensiveness requires that you deactivate your reactor button. You may initially feel hurt by what your partner says, because you are human and no one enjoys hearing about his or her imperfections. The key is to notice the hurt and recognize that you can feel it and still not have to operate from it. This will allow you to step outside of yourself to receive your partner's truth objectively, then assess clearly whether you think what he or she is saying is valid. If you do not think it is, then you can respond accordingly. If you do think your partner's comments have merit, you can use the information constructively toward your own improvement.

For example, Jamie was upset with Bob for leaving the house a mess for her to clean up when she arrived home from a business trip. When she confronted Bob, letting him know that she thought what he did was inconsiderate, his immediate reaction was to become defensive. Rather than hearing what Jamie had to say, he got angry because he felt he was being attacked. "I *always* keep the house clean," he retorted. "In fact, I usually have to clean up after *you*."

In order for Bob to listen to Jamie's feelings without defensiveness, he must take a step back from his initial impulse to react and simply hear what Jamie has to say. The key is for him to remember that listening to Jamie's point of view will not automatically invalidate his own. If he could have listened without reacting immediately, he might have been able to recognize that he was responding defensively because he was embarrassed at his lack of consideration.

Of course, this is much easier said than done. It requires the will-power to refrain from judging your partner's actions when they have a direct impact on you. Those are the moments you must choose in a split second whether to take a step toward intimacy by listening without judging or toward damage by reacting with defensiveness, anger, or criticism.

Let's look at Karen and Bill. Karen and Bill had just signed all the papers to finalize the purchase of their new home. It was two stories, with a backyard, ample room for the children, and proximity to shopping and schools. It was everything Karen wanted, but the moment she signed the papers, she felt sick. She was consumed by the feeling that they had made a dreadful mistake.

So many people fear having made an egregious error after making a significant purchase that this phenomenon has officially been named "buyer's remorse." Bill was clearly not feeling any such remorse, since he was smiling and shaking everyone's hands, elated that the loan had come through and delighted that they would finally be building a life together in their own home. Karen was afraid that the payments would be too steep for them and that they had gotten in over their heads. She was seized by panic that they didn't have enough money to adequately furnish the house and that perhaps the neighborhood was really not as safe as the realtor had said. She tried to hide her concerns rather than be a damper on Bill's enthusiasm.

While sitting in the car driving back to their apartment, Karen could no longer contain herself, so she took the risk: "Bill, I have to talk to you." Bill was wrapped up in his excitement and was clueless as to what she was about to say. "Sure, honey," he replied. "What is it?" Karen blurted out her truth: "I'm afraid that we may have made a terrible mistake."

This is the moment when the response either pursues intimacy or shuts down communication completely. If Bill reacts with anger, shock, judgment, or interrogation, then Karen will either close herself off, feel isolated, and/or become panicky. The situation will escalate into a full-blown argument, which will leave both of them distraught. If, however, Bill suspends his own reaction, reaches out to Karen with empathy, and says, "Tell me what's going on," chances are that Karen will open up, tell him her concerns no matter how difficult it might be, and together they can determine the best course of action. Often, it is in the mere telling that fears can dissipate. In this case, there is a good chance that just by giving Karen the opportunity and encouragement to air her truth, Bill allowed her fear to lessen and perhaps even disappear. He also took a step toward creating a deeper level of intimacy between them by strengthening the lines of communication rather than shutting them down with reactionary judgment.

NO STONES IN THE BASKET

Remember Lili and Charles, the couple who met on the rooftop and vowed to make communication the basis of their relating? Well, Lili shared with me what she calls her "No Stones in the Basket" rule, a ground rule I think is so important and valuable that I think it is worth passing along.

Lili explains it like this: We each carry a small, invisible basket around in our minds. In order to operate at maximum effectiveness as a human, it is best for that basket to remain empty and light, so as not to weigh us down, much like the Buddhists' ideal of a "Zen mind."

Occasionally, we might hold on to a feeling of resentment, anger, annoyance, or any other negative reaction, neglecting or refusing to release it to the person for whom it is intended, and that feeling turns into a stone. Each stone gets placed into the basket in our mind and remains there until we consciously choose to root it out and discard it.

The problem comes when people with heavily weighted baskets (and hence minds) try to pretend that all is just fine. No matter how hard they try, the rattling of those stones in the basket will distract them and clutter their thoughts. The weight of the stones will press down on them like a heavy burden, keeping them from optimal mobility. Hence, Lili explains, the goal is to keep your basket free of stones so that you can function without the handicap of a head full of rocks.

Each time you hold your tongue when your partner slights you, you create a stone. Each time you refrain from expressing a desire, the resulting resentment solidifies into another stone. Whenever you withhold your anger, yet another stone forms. You can see how little time it would take for your basket to become full and overflow onto your partner in the form of little jabs, heavy bombs dropping, sarcasm, loaded comments, and, when left unattended over time, explosions of emotional debris.

Some people consciously choose to hold on to their stones, polishing them into diamond-hard weapons. I know a woman whose husband was unfaithful, and rather than working through her feelings about it with him, she chooses to carry the stone around in her basket to hurl at him whenever the time is right. She continually makes the stone heavier by allowing her friends to add their indignation to it and refuses to let go of its hold over her and the ransom it demands—her husband's continual shame and punishment.

The goal in authentic unions is to toss out stones as quickly as possible when they appear. Keeping them around for any reason will do nothing but weigh down you and your relationship.

TELLING YOUR TRUTH

At the heart of the "No Stones in the Basket" theory is the cardinal commandment of *telling your truth.* You may believe that you could never tell your truth for fear of the consequences. If you withhold your truth because you believe that the other person can't handle it and will be hurt or angry or offended beyond repair, then you are doing her an even bigger disservice than you know. By withholding your truth, you not only weigh down your own basket, which affects her anyway, but you also deny her the opportunity to grow from your feedback.

Chloe had been dating Aaron for three years, and during the entire course of their relationship, she withheld her honest feelings about how she felt about Aaron's lovemaking. He was, as she described it, "clueless and inconsiderate" and as a result, she had difficulty responding to him sexually. The trouble spilled over into the rest of their relationship, as Chloe's resentment about this increased exponentially with each unsatisfying encounter.

Chloe eventually reached a point at which she knew she had to either speak her truth or end the relationship, since she was unwilling to live with an unsatisfying sex life. She finally told Aaron, and though he reacted badly at first out of wounded pride, he eventually expressed a desire to learn more about what she wanted and how to please her. This opened a door for them to a whole new level of connection, as they began to explore their sexuality together. They read books, explored new options, and even went to tantric sex seminars. With each new awareness, their lovemaking improved. They learned to have fun with their bodies and to honor each other's sacred sexual essence. Now, Chloe and Aaron have a sexual relationship that is mutually satisfying and has taken their union to a whole new level.

It is never easy to disclose your truth when you feel it might cause another person some pain. You might even need to wait for the weight of the stone to increase to a point that your head literally aches from it. Eventually, the burden of holding on to your truth will hopefully be greater than your tolerance to withstand it and you will need to take a deep breath and say your truth. The only other alternative is to exit the relationship.

If you need to cast out a stone but are afraid to, ask yourself what is the worst that can happen. By tracking this scenario to its extreme, you can shed light on the actual fear that is holding you back and then shrink it down to realistic size. For Chloe, her worst-case scenario was that she would tell Aaron how she felt and he would get so offended that he would walk out. She knew that would be devastating, but she also knew that she could survive, because she needed to be in the kind of relationship where truths could be exposed without fear.

Then comes the risk—the leap of faith that your relationship is strong enough to sustain this risk. If it doesn't, you will at least have already addressed the worst-case scenario and will know that this partner is not committed to creating a union at the same level of authenticity as you. It will hurt, of course, but no more or less than a head full of stones.

ASKING FOR WHAT YOU WANT

Nothing creates a stone faster than not asking for what you want. It is the quickest way for resentments to form, as it not only impacts your tangible reality but your self-respect as well.

Zoe and Richard have been a couple for nine years. Each time they go on vacation, Richard makes all the plans, books the tickets, sets the itinerary, and surprises Zoe with the trip as a done deal. Zoe pretends to be delighted each time, but secretly harbors a wish that Richard would allow her to choose where they went just once. She found it difficult to ask for this, since she did not want to appear ungrateful, and figured that since Richard financed the vacation, he should be entitled to choose where and how they traveled anyway. Yet each time Zoe remained silent, it chipped away at her self-esteem a bit more, as she silently seethed at her inability to ask for what she wanted.

It is not always easy to ask for what you want. Many people, like Zoe, fear that they will be perceived as demanding, which in their minds is a loathsome quality. Others may fear rejection or judgment about what they want ("you want *what?*"), or they might believe that they don't really deserve to get what they want.

If asking for what you want is difficult for you, you will need to first understand the underlying reasons why this is so before you can adopt new skills. If you believe that what you want does not matter, then I would recommend you loop back to Rule One and see where that belief is leading you. You may need to do some inner work so that you can rewire your thinking. You deserve to get what you want; if you believe that, it will make asking for it much easier.

If asking for what you want is difficult because you feel reticent or scared, then you will need to start small in order to retrain yourself. You can learn to exercise your "I want" muscle in little ways at first ("I want ice cream," "I do not want to watch that television show"). Like any muscle, its strength and capacity will build with use, until saying "I want" is no longer such a struggle. Eventually, you can work your way up to the bigger requests ("I want to go on a cruise instead of skiing," "I want to live in the city"). Let the important people in your life know you are working on this issue. When you alert people that you are trying to create a change within yourself, you align them with your goal and rally their support.

You can face the fears and beliefs that hold you back from asking and learn the needed skills to ask for what you want, ultimately creating the possibility that you will get what you want. Or you can cling to your limiting beliefs and atrophied "I want" muscle and live with a basket full of stones. The choice is yours.

———

Learning how to communicate with your partner is an ongoing process. It takes time, practice, and patience to keep the lines of communication open. With each new skill you acquire, however, you allow the energy in your relationship to flow with greater ease. Every disclosure of truth, effective exchange, and suspension of judgment brings you one step closer to your partner and to a deep and lasting connection.

NEGOTIATION WILL
BE REQUIRED

♥

*There will be times when you and your partner must work
through impasses. If you do this consciously and with respect, you
will learn to create win-win outcomes.*

For any two people to navigate their way through the journey of life together, negotiation is required. Negotiation is the process of sorting out what each person needs and wants and arriving at a solution that is satisfactory for both parties—creating what I call a "win-win outcome." Negotiation will be required when the differences between the two partners arise—as they invariably will—and when communication is not quite enough to get them through the impasses.

Although the term "negotiation" is most often used in business settings or financial transactions, you will find that the same princi-ples come into play in your relationship. The reason why profes-sionals use negotiation as a means of resolving differences is be-cause it is the most effective way to arrive at a fair solution. Negotiation is required any time two separate entities desire to come to an agreement in their relationship; it will be what brings you and your partner into alignment. Negotiation helps you ma-neuver through the emotional triggers, hot spots, and areas of dis-agreement with a rational and cool head.

The biggest surprise many people encounter when they enter re-lationships is to discover that relationships take time and effort. Falling in love is the wondrous part, but continuing to relate effec-tively day after day can, indeed, be challenging. In Rule Five we saw that to maintain the connection between two people, effective com-munication is absolutely essential. The step beyond communica-tion is negotiation. Negotiation is needed for partners to bridge their separate realities and shift back into alignment over and over again; negotiation is also required to work through impasses that will occur.

When two entities team up, they must make decisions and choices about their shared life. This can be challenging, mainly be-cause people don't always see eye to eye. When there are discrepan-cies in priorities, values, style, and preferences, negotiation will be required.

DEALING WITH DIFFERENCES

When two people come together, they will not have everything in common. Granted, in order to work, relationships demand that the partners have some measure of compatibility and shared interests. But it is very safe to assume that they will have differences that will need to be reconciled. There are so many areas for potential discrepancies to arise that it is amazing that any two people can really be a match at all.

You and your partner may have differences in lifestyle preferences. For example, Rick loves city life and Jeanette is drawn to the suburbs. Thomas prefers five-star hotels and Jillian likes to camp. Dylan enjoys the finer luxuries in life and Vanessa likes to live a simple life. Michel loves to dine in fancy restaurants and Dana would rather eat at the local pizzeria.

You may differ in how you like to spend your free time. Sonia likes foreign films, and Marv likes comedies. Burt is a workaholic, and Edna prefers touring resorts. Elaine loves water sports, and Marshall gets seasick. Patrick likes to watch basketball, and sports bore Marci to tears. Bonnie likes to scour flea markets, and Scott hates to shop.

You and your partner might differ in your needs. Maura needs a lot of private time, and Frank wants to be with Maura as often as possible. Tracy has a strong sex drive, while Ron would be content making love once a month. Natalie recharges by traveling, and Chris refuels by staying home with a stack of books.

Your personal tastes might not be in complete accord. Mel is a meat-and-potatoes man, and Dotty loves spicy ethnic food. Martin appreciates modern architecture, and Betsy loves Victorians. Tracy likes the symphony, and Bud is a rock and roll guy.

Your paces may differ. Sam walks quickly and purposefully, Lisa is more of a meanderer. Jordan is a morning person, and Jerry stays up until dawn. Wendy packs her datebook with social activities, and Elliott feels overwhelmed if he has more than one scheduled social plan per week.

Lastly, your priorities or philosophies may not be the same. Amy is conservative with finances, and Abe loves to buy drinks for everyone. Howie is a conservative Republican, and Vivian is a liberal Democrat. Alexander believes in God, and Annie is an atheist.

How can you deal with someone who is completely different from you in one aspect or another? By simply letting them be and resisting the impulse to change them into your clone. They are fine just the way they are.

So many people subscribe to the "diamond in the rough" theory, which makes them believe they can mold their partner into their vision of a shining gem. The human impulse to change others is strong, yet you cannot choose a partner based on what you believe you can transform that person into. What they like, what they need, and how they operate are all inherent in who they are as people. When you choose to be in a relationship with another, it is your responsibility to accept her as she is, right now.

For example, my husband and I are very different in the way we make decisions. I am very intuitive and make decisions quickly with very little data. Michael, on the other hand, requires a great deal of data before he will make a choice. You can imagine that shopping is an interesting experience for the two of us.

One afternoon we went shopping for a navy double-breasted blazer for him. I was ready to make a purchase after he had tried on the third one. I was ready to get on with our day. Michael, on the other hand, wanted to try on every available one in his size that was within a ten-mile radius. We both could have been judgmental about the other person's decision-making style and started a useless argument, but we chose not to. We solved our predicament like this: I realized that Michael was simply being Michael, and that trying to mold him into my image was not only futile but disrespectful to him. I released my position that speedy decision making is more desirable than a high need for data. At first, I thought he should hurry up and make his purchase but after I saw how silly my pressuring him was, I gave him full permission to do as much "research" that day as he wanted. I decided I was just there to spend the afternoon in his company.

I watched him try on more navy blazers that day than I ever imagined existed. He thoroughly enjoyed himself, and I enjoyed watching him have fun. He didn't purchase anything on that particular afternoon, which would have been unthinkable for me, but I let him do things his way and we both had a wonderful time.

Regardless of the origin or nature of your differences, you and your partner will need to find ways to make space for each person's wants and needs and to live harmoniously despite obvious variations in your individual tunes.

WORKING THROUGH IMPASSES

An impasse is a misalignment that results in a standstill. When you and your partner put forward your views or desires and you discover they are in opposition, then you will be faced with a choice: to either move into "needing to be right" or "wanting the outcome to work for both of us." The scenario you choose will determine whether you embark on an effective negotiation or a battle royal.

DISAGREEING VERSUS ARGUING

Couples disagree. That is as certain as saying the sky is blue. All couples, at one time or another, will have to grapple with opposing opinions, desires, or needs. What differentiates an authentic couple, however, is that they endeavor to sort out their differences and avoid letting their disagreements escalate into arguments.

An argument is similar to a disagreement in content but vastly different in intent. Disagreeing means holding opposing views. Arguing means holding opposing views and *investing energy into winning the other person over to your position.* When a disagreement escalates into an argument, the partners dig their heels in and take on the role of warriors seeking to best their opponent.

An argument carries with it the burden of righteousness. When you and your partner quarrel, one or both of you has an investment in being right. If being right is more valuable to either of you than working out a mutually satisfactory outcome, then you will remain locked in "fight mode" until one of you either gives up or wears down the other. Whoever dominates "wins" the argument. This is usually the person who yells the loudest, fights the hardest or the most cunningly, or wears down his partner with the most persistence.

Domination, winning, and losing are all terms of competition and warfare that would be better left on the playing field and battlefield than in the arena of love relationships. Yet so often couples employ them when disagreements arise, plunging themselves into bloody battles. While an argument might be a battle won for one person, it brings you both painfully close to losing a war.

Fights damage the connective tissue of your relationship. If hurtful words are exchanged in the heat of anger, the trust between you can get bruised. Hostile words can slice wounds deeper than any dagger. If you or your partner do not feel safe to disagree with the other, then opposing desires or needs may be suppressed, only to resurface later as resentments.

When Andre and Roberta started what seemed to be their millionth argument about finances, he angrily said to her, "You can't be trusted. You spend and spend; you're totally out of control. I should just take away all your credit cards and your checkbook because you can't handle money." These words cut through Roberta like a knife and she felt infantilized and demeaned. Andre may have felt like he was being honest, but the hurt that his words caused went quite deep and Roberta never forgot it.

It is okay to disagree. It is also permissible to argue at times. If you are fighting to resolve rather than fighting to win, then arguments can be a healthy way of releasing the emotions surrounding the disagreement.

What is unacceptable is hurting the one you love just to be right. Be careful what you say in the heat of passion. Focus on the issue at hand and remember that assassinating your mate's character will cause damage far greater than the satisfaction you may feel from getting your way in the moment.

WIN-LOSE OUTCOMES

In a win-lose outcome one partner gets what she wants at the expense of the other. One person (the "winner") successfully defeats the other (the "loser"). The winner walks away satisfied, while the loser may feel humiliated, beaten down, resentful, or abused. The victory may give gratification to one person, but it came at a significant price.

There is an exact moment when couples veer away from healthy negotiation into the win-lose dynamic. It is when the misalignment between the partners is put forth and one or both partners becomes attached to their position. Attachment causes partners to dig their heels in and clasp on to their position more vigilantly, which in turn polarizes the partners further. From within their polarized positions, the partners then begin "case-building," or gathering support for their positions and accumulating data that will discredit the other person. With both partners deeply entrenched in their need to be right, the only thing left to do is battle it out to see who is the more skilled at debating. This is *not* the ideal scenario for an authentic couple.

For example, Brian and Dede had strong opinions about everything. They were both stubborn and invested in their own ideas. Dede wanted to spend the holidays with her family. Brian wanted to get away with Dede alone, just the two of them. Every year, this same topic surfaced and they reran the same scene. The scenario went like this:

Dede brought up the subject. "I'd like to go spend the holidays with my family."

Brian replied on cue. "I thought this year we could get away by ourselves. Maybe go to an island resort."

Dede immediately felt the fear of losing surge in her. She knew that she wasn't going to be swayed and felt that she needed to build a solid, irrefutable case for her side. First she tried guilt.

"You know my parents are aging, and there may not be too many more Christmases that we have together," she said.

"Are you kidding?" Brian retorted. "With those genes in your family, they'll outlive all of us."

Dede tried a different tack. "It's so much fun when the whole family gets together. Good food, and it's always so great to see all the kids."

Brian of course did not agree. "Yeah," he bantered, "screaming kids, everybody stuffing themselves, and we all have to yell just to be heard above the noise. Tons of fun!"

Dede knew she was losing ground, so she tried reasoning. "It's the only time of the year that everyone is free to take the time to cook, talk, and catch up with each other. It's important."

Brian could sense that Dede was gaining on him, so he turned the tables and applied persuasion. "Just imagine us away from it all—drinking Mai Tai's on a sandy white beach under the warm sun. We could go snorkeling and sailing and take romantic walks in the moonlight. Now doesn't that sound like fun?"

Dede became frustrated and pulled out all the stops. "You don't care about me or my family. You're so selfish!" Brian, feeling wrongly accused, responded angrily, "You don't care about our relationship. You care more about your siblings than you do about me. Your priorities are all screwed-up!"

At this point, Brian and Dede have become polarized. They are both building cases for their points of view and working to discredit the other's. Name-calling, accusations, guilt, and persuasion are being used to make each of them right and their partner wrong, and inevitably feelings are getting hurt in the process.

The problem is twofold: first, neither person is being swayed over to the other person's side, and second, they are digging themselves deeper and deeper into their separate realities, which will make it nearly impossible for them to resurface in order to negotiate fairly. They are engaged in attack, defend, retaliate, and counterattack—a cycle that can escalate the argument into a major battle.

Throughout this ordeal, both of them are trying to "win" the argument and get their way, regardless of the effect it has on their partner. The problem is they are losing ground with each other. One person may, in fact, wear the other down, but if the rapport between them has been damaged, then has anyone really won at all? At a certain point, either Brian will concede and go to Dede's family and resent it, or Dede will give in and go to an island all the time wishing she were spending the holiday with her family. Neither of them is thinking clearly enough to find a creative win-win solution that could make them both happy. At this moment, they can only see the age-old win-lose option.

Brian and Dede never learned to negotiate, so each time this subject comes up, they immediately move into their disparate positions and defend them fiercely. They know how to compete and dominate, but not how to collaborate. What they will need to do to prevent this cycle from occurring again and again is learn how to ensure that both of them get what they want by negotiating win-win outcomes.

NEGOTIATING WIN-WIN OUTCOMES

A win-win outcome is one in which both people sincerely feel that they have each gotten what they wanted without giving anything up. Rather than the outcome being an "either or" scenario, it is an "and" scenario. For many people, this may seem more daunting a challenge than it really is. The reason so many people may think such an outcome is impossible is because they believe that when they and their partner have opposing views, that those views are *mutually exclusive.* Yet very often they are not.

Opposing views do not necessarily negate each other. If one person likes jazz and the other likes rap, that does not mean that only *one* person gets to listen to his music. Nor does it mean that *neither* gets to listen to her music. Rather, it means that they need to find a way for *both* people to be able to listen to the music they enjoy. There is always a way to make both people happy if you are willing to go through the process of negotiating a win-win outcome.

Negotiating win-win outcomes may feel challenging for some because most people enjoy being right, and they prefer to win rather than conceding to their partner's point of view. For many, compromise means to be weaker or inferior to your opponent. It means to give up what you want and settle for something that is less than you originally desired. However, in a win-win outcome, there is no concession, as both people walk away from the negotiation feeling gratified that both of them got what they wanted.

WHAT IS REQUIRED

To effectively negotiate a win-win outcome you will need to start by respecting your partner's needs and wishes. What your partner wants and needs is no less or more important than what you want or need. If you immediately debase the value of what your partner needs or wants, you begin polarizing before you even give the situation a chance to work harmoniously.

Sally loved soap operas, and she taped her favorite ones during the day so she could watch them in the evenings. Her partner, Dominick, thought watching television in general was a waste of brain cells and that there were far more stimulating things Sally could—and should—be doing with her time. He constantly asked her to turn the television off when he was home, often letting her know how ridiculous he thought this pastime of hers was. When Sally tried to create an arrangement with Dominick that would give him the quiet time he needed and would still allow her to watch her favorite shows, he scoffed at her and refused to even engage in the conversation. By not respecting Sally's desire, he shut down any effective negotiating before it could even begin.

You will need to arrive at the negotiating table with a willingness to listen to what your partner has to say. If you are so focused on your own wants, you will be unable to hear the specifics of what your partner wants. You will be frozen within the parameters of your position, unable to open your ears or your mind to new, alternative possibilities. You must possess a sincere desire to resolve the issue and move through the impasse. This desire will open your eyes so you can see a new paradigm of "our way" versus "your way" or "my way."

THE NEGOTIATION PROCESS

Negotiating a win-win outcome is not as difficult as you may think. Specific steps will get you from where you are to where you want to end up.

The first step is for you and your partner to disclose your needs or desires. This is when you both put the facts on the table to see if they are in alignment. If they are, then you have your outcome already. If they are not, you will need to move on to the next step.

The second step is assessing what your *shared* desired outcome of the situation is. You will need to come up with a statement that encompasses both people in agreement. The key is to find the overarching desire that is absolutely true for *both* people. Usually this requires that you look beyond the specific desire to the underlying purpose beneath it. For example, in Brian and Dede's case, their shared desired outcome would not be to go to Dede's family or to an island; rather, their shared desire might be something like "spending the holidays together in a way that allows us both to recharge harmoniously." Neither of them would be able to argue with this statement, and it would give them a platform from which they can work.

The third step is to lay out the different pieces of who wants what and why, and discuss how to make your shared desired outcome into a reality. The key question to ask is "What can we do so that you can have what you want *and* I can have what I want?" As you sort through the pieces, you move closer and closer to finding the creative solution that works.

If Brian explained that his goal was to have some private time with Dede so they could be romantic while also recharging his battery by being in the sunshine, then Dede would know what it was about the island vacation that was important to him. Conversely, if Dede explained that being with her family for Christmas was a spiritual and emotional experience for her, Brian would understand what Dede was yearning for. Perhaps they could work out an arrangement whereby they went to Dede's family for Christmas Eve and day, and then left on December 26th for the Bahamas. That way, Dede gets to spend the actual holiday with her family, and Brian gets to spend a wonderful week frolicking in the sun with his wife.

The Steps in Action

Claudia and Mark were ready to buy a new car. He wanted to buy a sport utility vehicle; Claudia was looking for a comfortable ride. Mark wanted something rugged; if it had been up to Claudia she would have put wheels on her living-room couch and traveled down the freeway in complete comfort. They were clearly not on the same page.

Claudia's first thought was, "He can get his own car, and I will get mine; that will solve the problem." Mark's response was, "Now don't go thinking that we are going to get two different cars because that's not in the budget." So her scenario of separating and splitting into two was not going to provide a solution. They would need to negotiate.

Mark and Claudia knew they did not want to do battle over whose car preference was superior. They had both enacted that scenario with other partners at other times, and neither wanted to go through the emotions that polarizing and hurting would cause. Though it was tempting to both of them to hold on to what each one perceived as the "right" choice, they both wanted to get through the car-buying process without either of them feeling resentful. Their statement of agreement was that they wanted to purchase a vehicle that would meet both of their objectives.

Mark and Claudia needed to see the exact areas where they were in agreement, and then relay to each other the specific priorities they had for their new car. They agreed that they needed to purchase a new car. They also agreed that they didn't want to spend over $15,000 on the vehicle, they both wanted to buy a preowned car rather than a new one, and they planned to own the vehicle for between one and two years. In addition, neither of them wanted to own a vehicle older than five years. They knew they didn't want a two-door, a stick shift, a van or a convertible, and black, white, red, and yellow were undesirable colors.

Once they had determined the areas of agreement, they could

then add into the mix what about their original choices attracted them. Mark said he wanted an SUV because of the way it handles, and that he liked the feel of a big vehicle. Claudia repeated her desire to have their new car be comfortable on the inside, so she could feel relaxed during long trips. As they laid out the different pieces, they were both able to see what was truly important to them and to their partner. Fairly quickly, they were able to construct a list of requirements that encompassed both of their needs. They could then start to build on their preferences and eliminate cars that didn't qualify.

They conducted their research and finally agreed on a car that both of them wanted. It was a sturdy vehicle that drove smoothly, handled well, and had a luxurious interior. Both felt satisfied and felt that they had not "lost." The secret to their successful negotiation was that they both softened their positions rather than becoming rigid about them, and were willing meet their partner in the middle. Although neither of them drove off in the vehicle that he or she had originally pictured, they were both happy with what they got. They were able to come to an agreement that encompassed all the points that were essential to each of them. The successful outcome came about because both partners scored a victory for their own needs without winning at the other's expense.

HOT SPOTS

There may be areas in your shared lives that cause difficulty again and again. These "hot spots" are situations that chafe each time they surface. For example, perhaps you and your partner have a different view of how three-day weekends and social situations should be spent. If you do not prenegotiate a win-win outcome for how to deal with this, there is a good chance that you will veer into a fight zone every time a similar situation arises.

Mallory had difficulty with the group of friends that her husband, Chuck, liked to socialize with from his law firm. Though she liked the men, she had some harsh judgments about their wives, all of whom had been part of this social group for years. Being around these women made her feel uncomfortable, as they seemed to go out of their way to make her feel excluded from their intimate circle. Yet because they were married to Chuck's friends, she often felt obliged to socialize with them. Whenever Chuck called to let her know there was going to be yet another company function, Mallory would tense up, and inevitably an argument would ensue.

Chuck's point was that not only were these his coworkers, with whom he needed to socialize for business reasons, but that they were also his friends. Mallory believed that Chuck should not ask her to continually put herself in social situations that made her uncomfortable. With every dinner party, company picnic, or other office gathering, the two of them would lock horns and get stuck in their respective positions.

Mallory and Chuck not only needed to learn to move this out of the realm of argument into negotiation, but they also needed to negotiate a win-win outcome that would hold true *each and every time this particular situation arose.* For maximum effectiveness, it would be best to negotiate this outcome while you are not actively engaged in the dynamic. By prenegotiating a fair way to deal with recurring differences, you will have an agreement that you can employ to solve the situation the moment it arises. The only way to diffuse hot spots is to anticipate their arrival and be equipped with a consistent, prenegotiated system for how to deal with them.

For example, Mallory and Chuck might discuss this situation at a time when no company event was pending, so they could be at their most rational and minimize the risk of running the same emotional patterns. Let's say the outcome they negotiate is that Chuck will ask Mallory to attend only those events at which her presence is truly important to him and excuse her from the others. At the events that she does attend, he will go out of his way to ensure that she feels comfortable. In exchange, Mallory will make her best efforts to go to the gatherings Chuck asks her to attend and do her best to have a good time. With that agreement in place, they would then be prepared for the next time they were invited somewhere with this group. They could both also refer to this agreement and be justified pointing out when and if the other deviates from the agreed-upon system.

Every couple has hot spots. However, knowing what causes them to erupt and negotiating their solutions in advance will help you work through these persistent impasses and enable you to spend your energy on building your relationship.

What are the hot spots in your relationship? Make a list and find time to discuss each one with your partner and negotiate a win-win situation.

Learning to live in harmony with another is not an easy task. You and your partner both came into the relationship with your own needs, desires, and views, and sometimes they may conflict. When differences arise, you will need to find ways to make your partnership a winning proposition for both of you. Within your "we" are two distinct "I" entities, both of which need to be heard and respected in order for your journey together to be a smooth one.

YOUR RELATIONSHIP WILL BE
CHALLENGED BY CHANGE

♥

Life will present turns in the road. How you maneuver those
twists and turns determines the success of your relationship.

*Y*ou can be certain of one thing in life: things will change. Change is the only constant we can count on. The entire universe is constantly in flux, and with each day, life presents us with new information and scenarios that we need to incorporate into our reality.

Often people resist the idea that they or their life circumstances will change. They enter relationships believing they will always feel as they do, and that life will always basically remain the same. Yet over the span of 10, 20, or 30 years, think of how much change you personally have experienced. Think of how different you are now from when you were 10, 30, or even 50. Now double that degree of change times two, since there are two people in your relationship, and you can see how important it is that you and your partner learn to deal with change effectively.

You and your partner will experience changes, both individually and collectively, throughout the course of your relationship. When your partner becomes your traveling companion through the journey of life, you will need to deal with the twists and turns that arise along your shared journey together.

Changes show up in many different forms. You can experience a change within the context of your career, your body, or your finances. A change can impact where you live or the size of your family. You could lose a loved one. Perhaps your emotions will shift, your priorities will shuffle, or your spiritual core will evolve. You and your partner may experience happy surprises and unexpected joys, as well as unanticipated hardships and sorrows. Regardless of what occurs, be it a challenge or a blessing, how you and your partner approach and handle change will reveal and test the bedrock that supports your union.

Change can either bring you and your partner closer together or it can drive you apart. Ultimately, the success of your partnership will depend on how you allow change to affect your relationship. In its worst form, change can cause you to step away from your commitment to go the distance, shaking your "we" reality. In its best form, it can build an impenetrable bond between you that will fortify your union and afford you deep and miraculous levels of intimacy. The choice is yours.

THE EFFECT OF CHANGE ON YOUR RELATIONSHIP

A change in the course of your time together shows up as what I call a "lifequake." Much like an earthquake, a lifequake is an event that causes tremors, possible damage, and ripple effects of shaky and unstable ground. When a lifequake happens, the reality you knew is altered, be it slightly or dramatically, and nothing is exactly as it was. The previous status quo has been rocked, and your relationship will need to have shock pads effective enough to absorb the impact.

PRESSURE ON YOUR FOUNDATION

Changes will apply pressure to the foundation of your relationship. How you cope with these changes together is a testament to the strength of your partnership and the level of joint cooperation. The power of "we" is tested in the face of new circumstances or crises; it is in those times that the "we" is reinforced through application.

It has been said that personal challenges are what build a person's character. By "character" we usually mean fortitude, perseverance, integrity, and the courage to stand up for your convictions. So, too, do challenges mold the character of relationships. Every relationship has a heart and soul all its own, and the changes that it must endure are what allow the heart's capacity to deepen and the soul to expand into greater realms. The amount of character that your relationship has will increase each time you survive yet another lifequake.

Nikki and Tom had a tumultuous year. First Tom lost his mother, then Nikki became pregnant and had a miscarriage. In between, Tom's company went public, which earned them a windfall of money, and Nikki was promoted to vice president. Each time they regained their emotional footing—positive changes need to be adjusted to as well as negative ones—another wave came and knocked them off balance again. Yet they made it through every trial and even managed to celebrate and incorporate some of the blessings. With each wave, they grew closer to each other, and they emerged from that year far stronger as a couple and more devoted to one another. While they certainly would rather have had a happier and less turbulent year, in the end, it was the best thing for their relationship.

The durability of your foundation will be tested, as the shock waves of change permeate the emotional bedrock below. All changes, both positive and negative, cause wear and tear. Each one will be a test of your patience, tolerance, and your ability to communicate, negotiate, and share. The durability of your foundation provides you with the ability to deal with change, and it keeps your relationship stable in the midst of lifequakes.

TEST OF YOUR COMMITMENT

Change will test your commitment. Once you are committed to a relationship, it is easy to maintain that commitment when factors within the relationship are stable, familiar, and comfortable; you have a perception that you are in control of your reality. You know what is expected of you and you are happy in your designated role.

It is not difficult to stay committed when you know the exact scenario that you are committed to. It is when that scenario shifts that you will be called upon to reexamine your initial choice to commit to your partner and to reassess your willingness to go the distance.

Mary and Simon were married. While they were on their honeymoon, Simon was in a car accident. The doctors did all they could, but he was paralyzed from the waist down. He would have to spend the rest of his life in a wheelchair.

Mary was faced with a change that she had not bargained for. However, she was only days away from her marriage vows to love Simon "for better or for worse, in sickness and in health." It took some time for her to adjust her vision of what her marriage would look like, but when she reminded herself that she loved Simon for his essence, not for his ability to walk, there was no question in her mind.

When a gap arises between how you imagined life would be and how it actually turns out, your level of commitment will be tested. Can or will you go the distance, even though the course is different from the one you anticipated? Not an easy question to answer, but one that you will be required to consider when changes arise.

HOW TO DEAL WITH CHANGE

As a management consultant and facilitator, I often work with companies to teach their executives and employees how to successfully manage change. Between mergers, acquisitions, expansion, downsizing, new technology, and divesting based on global economics, companies are constantly changing. Business leaders know that in order to ensure the company's success, they need to pay close attention to how the changes are incorporated into the infrastructure of their organization and give their employees the information and tools with which to transition smoothly. What companies need in order to successfully deal with change is a solid structure, the flexibility to incorporate new initiatives, and the resources to make it work.

The process for dealing with change in love relationships is not so different. Granted, love relationships harbor a level of vulnera-bility and emotionality that may not be present or acknowledged in the workplace. However, the basic underlying process of how to deal with change actually remains exactly the same.

To maneuver through changes successfully, you both will need to begin with the three basic requirements: a strong foundation, flexi-bility, and the specific tools to work through the change process. Your foundation is what grounds you, and your flexibility is what will allow you to bend and bounce back, rather than break. The steps for how to deal with change give you the resources to guide and support you through the process, so you can manage change in a constructive, satisfying manner.

A STRONG FOUNDATION

Life evolves, issues arise, and circumstances shift. The key to surviv-ing the passage of time and the changes that come along is a rock-solid foundation. How you communicate, cooperate, and process with each other is the true basis of your relationship and what will ultimately determine how you collectively weather both storms and sunshine. As W. Mitchell, one of my dear friends, says, "It's not what happens to you, but what you do about it that matters."

A young man named Adam came to me right before he was mar-ried. I was scheduled to be the minister, and he figured I would be the right person to come to with his growing concerns. He was nervous about his ability to go the distance and seemed uncertain about how to wrap his mind around the "for better or for worse" part of his upcoming vows. He mentioned that his parents had divorced while he was still a child. I asked him to tell me the story, sensing that it was relevant to Adam's current fears.

His father, Donald, was a wealthy man when he met Tara, Adam's mother. Tara's family had struggled financially all her life, and Donald offered her not only affection but a chance to live the lifestyle she had always dreamed about. Tara was also extraordinarily beautiful, and Donald was captivated by her dark hair and stunning face. They married six months from the day they met.

Donald and Tara settled into a life that worked for both of them, albeit superficially. Tara enjoyed her newfound luxuries and financial freedom, and Donald liked showing off his raven-haired bride. Tara's self-image was boosted by Donald's attention, and their exchange of needs seemed to be a neat fit. Adam was born a year after they were married—an event which they shared in appearance but not in spirit. The first ten years of the marriage passed, and though their relationship was not emotionally intimate or truly authentic, neither of them had any complaints.

Then crisis hit. The market crashed and Donald's business went under. They were forced to drastically alter their lifestyle, which caused much tension between them. They had no joint coping mechanisms, so they each dealt with the situation privately. Just as they were getting back on their feet, Tara was told that the small mole on her cheek was malignant and would need to be removed. The surgery took care of the problem but left her with a noticeable scar.

All the factors converged, and Donald and Tara's foundation succumbed to the pressure. With Donald's feelings of guilt, Tara's damaged self-image, and their collective inability to build a new foundation on factors other than financial freedom and physical beauty, their marriage did not stand a chance.

I told Adam it was not surprising that he worried about his bride and he withstanding change, given the background from which he came. Yet even in the mere retelling of the story, Adam was able to see how much different he and his fiancée were from his parents. They had a foundation that was built on trust, honesty, and the open exchange of thoughts, ideas, feelings, and fears. He and I agreed that that would be what would enable them to go the distance "for better or for worse." As he and his new bride stood before me at the altar, I could almost feel the strength of the bond between them, and I knew they had what it takes to survive the changes that life brings.

FLEXIBILITY

A strong foundation is your core, but you will also need flexibility to withstand the bumps in the road. Think of riding a roller coaster: if you tense every muscle, you will hit the sides of the car and exit the ride sore and bruised. If you relax, breathe, and go with the motion, you will enjoy the ride far more and probably disembark unharmed.

My husband and I wear wedding bands that are constructed of gold chain links that bend and conform to the contours of our fingers, rather than solid bands. We chose these rings as a symbol of our bond: strong and durable, yet flexible enough to withstand change. Those rings serve to remind us every day that we need to stay connected yet flexible for our relationship to endure the ups and downs of life.

Being flexible requires that you be unattached to *what was*. Each time a change occurs, *what was* ceases to exist and *what has become* is the norm. Change signals a new chapter. Flexibility is what allows you to be quick on your feet rather than digging in your heels and clinging to what you once knew.

Francine and Greg had been married for twelve years when Francine decided to start her own business. She kept telling Greg that everything within their relationship would stay the same, and he believed her. Once she started the business, however, the demands on Francine's time were intense. She rarely made it home for dinner anymore—a ritual that she, Greg, and their two children had previously been diligent about. She spent many weekends working, rather than out on their boat with the family. Those rare weekends that she was free, she was generally too exhausted to do anything but relax. Though Francine tried to keep up with her responsibilities within the family, she found it difficult to get everything accomplished, and frequently felt overwhelmed.

Greg resented the amount of time Francine's new business consumed. He missed the time with his wife and worried that they were drifting apart because they rarely had time together anymore. He also felt resentful that he inherited her tasks and management of the household, as well as the caretaking of their children. He preferred life the way it was before Francine started her new venture.

They argued frequently, and because she felt guilty, Francine pushed herself harder to get home in time for dinner, which meant she would spend the rest of the evening in her study completing her work from the day. She made the effort to join Greg on their boat more often. This continued until one day Greg looked over and saw Francine sitting at the dinner table, dozing off.

The situation had gone far enough. Both Greg and Francine were so attached to their previous way of life that neither of them had embraced their new reality. They finally admitted this to themselves and each other, and they agreed that the situation required them to be flexible and to renegotiate their relationship, rather than rigidly trying to make the new pieces fit into the old design.

Change is not a temporary thing. You do not pass through it and then return to normal. What was normal has been altered, either slightly or radically, and you will need to accommodate whatever new elements are called for into your shared life in order to make it run smoothly again.

PROCESSING CHANGE

Change comes in different ways. It can happen to one of the partners, as when one person loses her job or experiences a health crisis. Change can also happen to both of you, for example when you move into a new home or have a child. Or you may need to deal with the results that occur when one partner goes through some sort of personal or spiritual evolution, for instance when one person chooses to return to school or decides to change his philosophy or religion. Regardless of how change comes, or who brought it about, it will be your shared responsibility to process its effect on your relationship and negotiate a new game plan.

Kurt Lewin, one of the fathers of organizational development, designed a model of change that is comprised of three parts: freezing, unfreezing, and then refreezing. The first part, freezing, represents the stage before change occurs. This is when the status quo is in place, and things feel predicable, familiar, controlled, stable, and certain. There is a clear understanding about what is expected from each person, how the dynamic between them operates, and what makes their life together run smoothly. The word generally used to define this phase is "normal," because norms have been established and are solidly in place.

The second phase of the change process is the unfreezing, or melting, stage. This is when the lifequake hits and the pieces of your shared life are flying about in all directions. Life becomes unpredictable, unstable, unfamiliar, unclear, uncertain, and uncontrolled. As a result, it appears disrupted, disorganized, and disturbing. The shock waves cause your foundation to tremble, and the handrails that you once held on to are no longer firmly in place. Your commitment and your tolerances are tested. The level of chaos is directly proportionate to the severity of the impact.

The third phase of change is the refreezing phase. This is when new norms have been established. In this phase, you set about repairing any damage caused by the lifequake and build new handrails to hold on to. The bedrock beneath you settles as feelings of familiarity, predictability, and control are once again restored.

Surviving the Meltdown

Phase one, the frozen stage, is not very challenging because things are the way they have been. It does not take a great deal of perseverance or creativity to cope with the status quo. Phase two, the unfreezing stage, is when the meltdown occurs and the real work begins. When things begin to change, everything you have learned up until that point will be tested.

There are two steps involved in jointly managing the melting process: disclosure and renegotiation. The first step, disclosure, requires that you and your partner convene and share your internal realities. You need to be clear and honest with each other about what is really going on and share how the change is affecting each of you. For example, Francine and Greg, the couple who needed to learn flexibility, could not effectively cope with the change that was occurring until they disclosed the truth of what was actually happening between them and how each of them felt about it. When Francine admitted that she was run-down and Greg shared his feelings of abandonment, the different pieces began to appear clearly before them. They could then move on to the second step: putting the pieces together in a new configuration through renegotiation.

Renegotiating is no different from regular negotiation, except that it requires you to release your attachment to your original outcome and be willing to work out and adopt an alternative. You will need to assess the situation, examine all the elements before you, and then work together to map out a new strategy that functions for both of you.

By going through the steps of disclosure and renegotiation, you and your partner can survive the meltdown process and establish new paradigms. It may take some patience, but eventually new norms will begin to feel as familiar and comfortable as the old ones did. You can almost count on the fact that once the norms settle in, another lifequake will occur and you will need to assess and renegotiate all over again. Change is a constant that we must learn to manage and grow from the process.

A Survival Story

Ross and Meredith tried unsuccessfully to have children. After years of tests and many experimental methods, the doctors could not find anything medically wrong with either of them. They very much wanted to be parents, so they finally decided to adopt a child.

They adopted a beautiful baby girl and named her Joy, to

represent the happiness she brought into their lives. But like any new baby, Joy also brought with her hilarity and chaos. She turned their lives upside down. Ross and Meredith remained as cheerful as possible as they learned to juggle dual careers, diapers, and 3:00 A.M. feedings. The new addition was a change they needed to adjust to. Just when they seemed to have everything under control, Meredith discovered she was pregnant—with twins! This happens so frequently that the adoption counselor was hardly surprised.

In their life design, Ross and Meredith had never counted on having three children, not to mention three children in diapers simultaneously. How would they care for three babies? How could they keep their income flowing if one of them needed to stay home to care for the children? *Where had they put that pacifier?* Their lives were scrambled, including their home, their finances, their schedules, and their emotions.

Ross and Meredith were in the midst of the meltdown process. They knew they needed to work together in order to survive the move from familiar to unfamiliar. They sat down at their kitchen table and talked through all the thoughts, feelings, and concerns that surfaced for both of them. Then they listed all the elements that needed adjusting, and they tried to anticipate what they would need to do in the coming months to survive. Using their communication and negotiation skills, they mapped out a game plan so that the new phase of their life could run as smoothly as possible.

The twins were born, and Meredith and Ross are now actively putting their new paradigm into play. Each day is a challenge, but they happily face it knowing that their new familiarity consists of chaos and joyful episodes of hapless uncertainty.

FACING LIFE TOGETHER

You and your partner are a team. What that means is that you will need to work together and to dance the steps of change in tandem. Where one is weak, the other can be strong; when one is damaged, the other can offer healing; when one has doubt, the other can provide faith. There is a natural cadence of "you–me–we" that establishes the rhythm of your dance. Keeping the beat of this rhythm when changes knock you off balance is what will bring you back into harmonious flow.

COPING WITH HARDSHIPS

Unfortunately, things happen. Life may deal you or your partner an unexpected hand, and the challenges that result must be handled. There are only two choices that couples have when hardships occur: to pull together or to pull apart. Pulling together means working as a team to process the thoughts and feelings and work out a strategy for dealing with the situation. Pulling apart means you each withdraw into your shell and abandon the "we" reality.

Adversity and crises bring out what you and your partner are made of, both individually and jointly. They might bring out panic in the form of "I can't," or selfishness with both partners looking out only for themselves. Or, they might stimulate both partners' stamina and deepen their commitment, allowing them to go the distance together.

If your partner loses her job, will you panic at the loss of income and cause her to do the same? Will you assume it is her problem to deal with and leave her on her own to cope? Or will you rise to the occasion and support her emotionally while helping her map out a game plan for exploring her options? Conversely, if you lose your own job, will you panic and spiral into "I can't," unable to do what is necessary for your joint financial survival? Will you retreat into your private world and shut out your partner? Or will you reach out to your partner for understanding and ask for his support? However you choose to handle either situation is a testament to what you are made of.

When adversity or crisis hits, regardless of how minor or major it registers on the seismograph, you and your partner will need to work through the emotions and the panic and pull together if your relationship is to survive the blow. When Jill was diagnosed with breast cancer, her immediate reaction was to withdraw from her husband, Anthony. Though the doctors were fairly certain she would be all right once they removed the tumor, she could not bear the idea of losing her breast and becoming physically incomplete to her mate. Her response was to pull away from Anthony.

The surgery was successful, but the emotional healing process took much longer. It took significant effort and patience on Anthony's part to coax Jill back into the safety of their intimacy. He spent many days worrying about whether they could survive the repercussions of Jill's surgery, yet he held on to his faith in their bond and persevered. It was his faith that carried Jill through; his faith eventually enabled her to turn toward him and allow him to support her.

As Jill and Anthony discovered, when you and your partner hold fast to each other as you round the hairpin turns on the winding road of life, your relationship deepens. If you move away from each other, the balance is jeopardized and you could veer off the road into the abyss below.

Challenges, hardships, and crises will happen, so it is best to use them as opportunities to strengthen your bond. Pulling together in crises is what partnership is all about, and it is what will enable you and your partner to move into greater realms of intimacy.

SHARING JOYS

When something wonderful happens to one of you, the joy belongs to you both. The spirit of teamwork means that you share in each other's glories, just as you commiserate with each other's defeats. Remembering to share the joy from positive changes is no less important than supporting each other through difficult patches.

At times, dealing with positive changes is just as challenging as dealing with negative ones. For example, Darci and Jack had been together for 17 years when Jack's newspaper column was picked up by a national syndicate. Up until then, they had enjoyed moderate success and were quite happy living a simple life. Jack became an overnight success and soon began appearing as a guest on talk shows and being interviewed on late-night programs. His fans increased daily, and since his photo ran next to his byline, people started recognizing him on the street.

The leap in Jack's career was, of course, a welcome change, but it was a change nonetheless and needed to be dealt with as such. He and Darci needed to pay attention to what the change meant for them, not just financially, but also how it impacted their time together, their privacy, and the dynamic between them. They needed to openly and honestly admit the shift in Jack's availability, and adjust their relationship so that Darci did not feel excluded from his success or left behind. Though the unfreezing phase would lead to greater financial freedom for them and personal fulfillment for Jack, it still created upheaval that needed to be addressed and handled with care.

If good fortune smiles upon you, it is right action to remember to include your partner in your experience. If the positive change happens to your partner, then you will need to adjust right along with them and make room for their new burst of growth while still leaving space for you. If something wonderful happens to you both as a couple, then you will need to embrace the new pieces together and incorporate all the joy into your shared reality.

If you could take a picture of your life as it is right now and freeze it for eternity, it might be great for antiquity, but the stagnation would eventually grow tiresome. Change is what makes life interesting and keeps people and relationships continuously evolving.

In order for you and your partner to go the distance, you will need to prepare whenever possible for the changes ahead. While you cannot anticipate all the lifequakes that will occur, you can plan for turns in the road by continually strengthening your foundation and developing an effective processing mechanism. That way, the changes that occur will feel less like events to worry about and more like opportunities to embrace.

YOU MUST NURTURE THE
RELATIONSHIP FOR IT TO THRIVE

♥

Treasure your beloved and your relationship will flourish.

a relationship is like a garden. If you tend to your garden with care, attention, and maintenance, it will grow. Give it plenty of sunshine and water, and the seedlings will mature into strong, healthy plants. Neglect it and hope for the best, and it will become overrun with weeds. Step on the plants, tear their leaves, deny them love and nutrients, and they will wither and die.

If you treat your relationship with appreciation and respect, it will remain strong. If you give it your time, attention, and effort, it will continue to grow with each passing day. However, if you take it for granted and assume it will just continue along as it is, chances are it, too, will wither and die.

It can be so easy to take a love relationship for granted. Once the "hard part" of finding and creating love is done, many people then declare themselves "set," and turn their attention to other areas; they check it off their list of things they need to do. A relationship, however, is an ever-evolving entity that demands nurturing in order to survive; like a garden, it has basic requirements. When the first harvest season is over, it still needs to be cared for with love, appreciation, and respect if it is to continue to bloom year after year.

Nurturing the connection between your partner and you is what sustains your relationship. That connection must be reinforced each and every day to remain strong. This reinforcement is not something only to be done annually, on anniversaries or birthdays, but rather it must become as normal to you as waking up in the morning and brushing your teeth. It is easy to feel this magic in the beginning of your relationship, when passions are high and emotions are flowing. The challenge is to maintain it through daily sustenance and nurturing of each other.

At the heart of nurturing your relationship is the act of treasuring your beloved. Treasuring your beloved means that you hold him dear to you. It means that you appreciate him for all his wonderful qualities and demonstrate as often as you can how important and special he is to you. In the act of treasuring, you show your partner in direct and subtle ways that he is the person who still makes your heart race and your stomach flutter. You show him that he contributes to the beauty of your life.

BEING FULLY PRESENT

According to Woody Allen, 90 percent of life is about just showing up. However, "just showing up" is not enough when it comes to love. There is a distinct difference to being there and *being there*. Being there means you are present and accounted for in physical form. *Being there* means you show up not just in body but in mind, heart, and spirit. It means that you are actively engaged in relating with your partner, and it means that you are fully present.

So many couples I have facilitated experience difficulties because one or both of the partners has chosen to numb out, retreating from the other, and ceasing to treasure her mate. This happens when something causes one or both people to lose the desire or energy to keep the relationship authentic and thriving. It can be an unspoken resentment, an unforgiven hurt, a waning of physical desire, laziness, or just the weightiness of life that drives them into their personal and private shells. They have fallen into a routine of neglect and hence have drifted miles apart. The gulf between them widens with each missed opportunity to connect—when one comes home and does not bother to embrace the other, when they walk past each other in their own home and fail to acknowledge the other with even the smallest gesture, when they cease disclosing to one another their feelings, or when they become too preoccupied with daily life to keep their sexuality alive. Eventually, they wake up and find themselves emotionally isolated in the context of their relationship.

When you move from being fully present to just showing up, you digress from the original "we" that you formed with your partner. You pull back from your union and retreat into your "I" state, setting up an impenetrable fence around you. You close your partner out of your reality, and your relationship suffers.

The way back from this digression is through rewinding the videotape of your mind. You will need to refer back to those times when you were fully present with your partner as a way to trigger your cellular memory. When you call up the feelings from those precious moments when you were truly *there* in heart, body, and spirit, your temporary amnesia will dissolve and you will find your way back to being fully present.

WAKING UP AGAIN

Joseph and Vera had been married for 22 years when Vera came to see me. She was unhappy because Joseph had been, as she described it, "emotionally absent" for the past ten years of their marriage. It seemed that Joseph simply stuck to his solitary routine of going to work, coming home, and settling into the couch with the remote control in his hand, night after night. Vera tried to reach him in various ways, but she could not seem to get Joseph to see how far apart they had drifted.

I suggested to Vera that she think of a memory in which Joseph was fully present. She immediately responded by telling me about a wonderful vacation that they had taken to an island a couple of years before. I suggested that she go home, turn off the television, and remind Joseph of that trip in vivid detail—how the breeze felt against their skin, what the moon looked like, the wonderful meal they ate by the water, how much in love they felt—so that his own version of this memory could surface. By juxtaposing that vivid and precious memory against where they were at present, Joseph might be able to see how far he had drifted from his beloved.

Vera went home, sat next to Joe, and asked him if they could talk during the next commercial break. He nodded in agreement. When the commercials came, she asked Joseph to mute the sound and face her. She then said, "How are you?" Joe gave his usual response of, "Fine," only this time Vera responded with, "Do you remember when we were on the island two years ago? Do you remember the feel of the breeze, and how we had a picnic on the beach? Remember how we drank piña coladas, and how well we slept? Do you remember how things felt between us?" Joseph responded that he did, indeed, remember. Vera then replied, "I would like to have that feeling back—and I think we can—but I need to know if you want it, too."

It worked. Joseph understood what Vera was saying when she explained that she felt far away from him. Together, they agreed that they needed to create some new precious memories so Joseph could stay awakened to their love.

CHECKING IN WITH EACH OTHER

Often couples get so caught up in their daily lives—jobs, errands, stresses, children, activities—that they forget that their relationship needs tending. Life gets busy, and when the demands of everyday existence take up all the spare moments, people can easily go unconscious and move into either "coast" or "cope" mode. They put so much time and effort into keeping all their plates spinning in the air that nurturing their relationship seems like the last thing they have time for. But one neglectful moment turns into hours, hours into days, and days into months, and before they realize how much time has passed, they are miles apart.

Things change, people change, and moods change. It would be silly to assume that the way things were last week is the way they will be today, or in a month from now. Since change is the norm, it is important to check in with each other about where each person is with himself and with the status of the relationship. Checking in wakes you from your unconscious state and reminds you of your primary connection to your beloved.

Checking in with your partner is comparable to taking your car in for a tune-up. After you drive your car for a certain number of miles, you bring it to the shop to have the brakes, plugs, oil, filter, and engine inspected in order to make sure everything is running properly. If anything is not as it should be, the problem is detected and repaired.

Relationship check-ins are tune-ups for your union. When partners check in, it means they set aside a few moments to touch base and connect with one another. Are they happy? Did they solve that problem at work? How are they feeling about themselves? You share with each other the joys, sorrows, challenges, breakthroughs, stresses, and victories that occur in each of your individual lives. You discover your partner's concerns and you share yours. You update each other on your current priorities and what has changed, both intrinsically and extrinsically, since you last touched base. In essence, checking in means pausing amidst your busy life to ask your partner with sincerity, "How are *you*?" and truly listening to the answer.

Checking in is taking the pulse of your relationship. It is important to share your thoughts and feelings about the status of your partnership so that you and your partner can stay connected. Are your expectations being met? Do you have any stones that need to be tossed from your basket? Do you feel secure? Appreciated? Taken for granted? Do you want to change anything regarding how you relate to one another? In order to keep a relationship authentic, it is necessary to pause every once in a while and ask "How are *we?*" Please be advised that "Fine" is not an acceptable answer.

EVERYDAY CHECK-INS

There are two kinds of check-ins—the everyday kind and the formal kind. Everyday check-ins occur when you and your partner stop whatever you are doing, even for one brief instant, and focus your attention on one another. This is when you consciously press "pause" and take a moment to realign yourself with what your partner is feeling, how his day is going, and what is on his mind.

Years ago it was customary for families to gather around the dinner table each night to share with each other events of the day and progress reports on their various life pursuits. Generations of couples believed that this was an important part of the day. Thus, for many couples, there was no need to establish any kind of checking-in system, because it happened automatically almost every evening over pot roast and mashed potatoes. However, times have changed, and establishing new routines for checking in with each other may be required.

Every couple has its own rhythm and habits. For example, Sidney and Jeri go to the gym together every weekday morning. Larry and Clay call each other throughout the day to report news, updates, or other points of interest. John and Camaryn have a standing dinner date every Wednesday night.

What works for you and your partner? Do you generally take a few moments before going to sleep at night to catch each other up on news, plans, thoughts, feelings, concerns, or breakthroughs? Do you like to meet for lunch one day a week? Perhaps you might prefer having coffee together in the morning or driving to work together. Whatever time, place, or method works best for you is appropriate; the only essential feature is that you discover what works for both of you and stick with it. The small amount of time and effort it takes will pay you back your investment many times over.

FORMAL CHECK-INS

A formal partnership check-in is a scheduled meeting at which past, present, and future issues are raised and sorted through. In this meeting, partners share their well-being, physical and emotional; they can share the issues they are addressing, the lessons they are learning, the triumphs and trials they are experiencing. They share about blocked areas, and ask for whatever support they need. After the personal side has been covered, they move into the interpersonal realms.

Both people have the opportunity to honestly address where they are in terms of the relationship. This needs to include both the good and the bad news—in other words, what's working and what's not working. Checking in with each other dissolves any assumptions that may have formed and puts you and your partner back on the same page.

You may be wondering why it is necessary to be so ceremonious about checking in. The main reason for this is because making your formal check-ins an event lends an air of credibility and meaning to them. Changing the tone of the encounter from casual to significant predisposes the partners to take it seriously and to carve out the time and mental energy to prepare in advance. Formal check-ins can be enormously helpful tools for adjusting your relationship so both people feel treasured as they should.

When you discuss your relationship, you may want to cover some of these points:

1. Overall feelings about the relationship:
   a. Are you getting your needs met?
   b. Are you speaking up and asking for what you want?
   c. Are you feeling heard?
   d. Are you feeling encouraged and supported to grow?
2. The decision-making process:
   a. Are decisions made to your satisfaction?
   b. Is there sufficient time to discuss, assess, and process?
   c. Do you feel as though your thoughts and feelings are taken seriously?
   d. Is there a collaborative spirit about decisions?
3. Communication:
   a. Do you feel safe to say whatever you feel?
   b. Do you feel listened to when you communicate?
   c. Do you feel encouraged to tell your truth?

      d. Do you feel supported in all your dreams and goals?

4. Roles and responsibilities:

      a. Do you feel the division of tasks is working?

      b. Do you feel that both of you are doing your parts?

      c. Do you feel that task allocation is fair?

      d. Is there anything that you want to change?

5. Activities:

      a. Do you feel like you spend enough time together?

      b. Do you feel like you need more alone time?

      c. Do you want to try something new?

6. Planning, schedules, and logistics:

      a. Are you experiencing any schedule conflicts you want to address?

      b. Are there financial agreements that are fair?

      c. Do each of you have enough time to accomplish everything you want?

An official check-in needs to be approached with a certain level of respect. As such, it is important that you both allocate enough time and that you conduct your meeting in the appropriate atmosphere. Discussing such important issues in the middle of the kitchen with the phone ringing, the children yelling, and the oven timer buzzing is not necessarily the most conducive way to achieve your goal of realigning. Nor is attempting to talk when one or both of you is stressed or worried about something else.

    Choose a time and a place that works for both of you. Find a private space for your partner and you to talk, at a time when you are both relaxed and can focus on each other. It is best if you can give your questions and answers some thought in advance, so you can be prepared and so that you remember to bring up everything on your mind. Good places are on long rides in the car, walks on the beach, or strolls in the park.

You and your mate need to determine how often and how officially you want or need to take the pulse of your relationship. It is really up to the two of you to pause and take stock of how things are going.

POSITIVE AND NEGATIVE ATTENTION

In the beginning of any relationship, exchanges between two people are warm, loving, and endearing. Sweet words of love flow effortlessly:

"You have beautiful eyes."

"I love the way you look in blue."

"It's such fun going to the gym with you."

"You make the best omelets!"

These phrases flow from a very natural and true place inside each individual. Each time one person offers positive attention to the other, it is like shining sunlight onto a flower. The recipient blossoms.

Appreciation begets more appreciation, the response is mutual admiration, and the recipient responds by showering love back on the giver. Positive attention is contagious, and a spiral is created that expands upward in the reciprocity of the exchange. This is, of course, the honeymoon stage.

Eventually, the rose-colored glasses are removed and reality sets in. At some point, the partners' "best self" slips, and they relax into a less perfect and less polished state. Suddenly, "oh wow" transforms into "oh no," and they each begin to realize that this other, perfectly marvelous person has flaws. Critical eyes start to notice these faults and point them out just in case the partner was unaware of them; the flow of positive recognition and attention now shifts toward more pointed or critical observations. Almost out of nowhere, criticism, sarcasm, and irritation creep into their exchanges:

"You left the top off the toothpaste again."

"Can't you clean up your clutter?"

"For once could you please fill up the car and not return it to me on empty?"

"That sweater is too small for you."

Tolerance is diminished, and declarations of frustration or annoyance eclipse words that were once sweet. The honeymoon is over.

What happened? What changed? Quite simply, the positive attention has turned into negative. The partners still focus their energy on one another, except that rather than expressing kind words, the exchanges are tinged with hostility. The upward spiral is reversed and degenerates into a downward corkscrew cycle: criticize, defend, retaliate, and so on until the partners can no longer see the parts of each other that they once thought so precious. This is not the healthiest way to relate, but it is the most common.

FROM NEGATIVE BACK TO POSITIVE

If you want your relationship to flourish, you will need to retrain yourself to focus on your partner's positives rather than her flaws. You will need to imagine your partner as perfect *exactly as she is*. After all, that is how you felt when you first met her. Think back to that time, and imprint in your mind the memory of how you viewed your partner in the beginning, when everything she did seemed acceptable—even marvelous. That is not to say you should overlook those aspects of your partner that you do not like; but rather, as you did when you met, you need to focus on what you *do* like about them and not dwell on those things that you *do not* like.

Maintaining that mind-set is like remembering to water the plants. It means recalling your initial choice to partner with your dear one, remembering why you chose that person in the first place, and refocusing on those qualities that made you fall in love. A young man I know has an elderly friend who always tells him to pause in those moments that he feels especially loving toward his wife and to make a list of the qualities he appreciates about her. That way, whenever she annoys, angers, or frustrates him, he has that list to refer to to keep himself aligned with his true feelings.

What is needed to reverse a negative corkscrew back to a positive spiral is for one person to step out of the cycle and change the energy. This requires one person stopping for a moment, consciously tapping into his memory of what he loves about his partner, and choosing to focus on that rather than on what he does not love. From there, he can shift his attention from criticism to appreciation. Since appreciation begets more appreciation, chances are his partner will respond in kind and the spiral will be back on track.

A Sample Spiral

Carey and Andy met and began dating exclusively almost immediately. They were blissfully enraptured with one another, and their honeymoon phase included little love notes of affection tucked into each other's coat pockets, an endless stream of compliments back and forth, and almost constant acknowledgment of each other's positive qualities. Carey loved the way Andy expressed himself, and Andy loved the way Carey listened so intently to his words. Carey liked the way Andy dressed, and Andy adored Carey's blond, curly hair. The list went on, and neither was shy about reciting from it often.

Six months into their relationship, Andy and Carey moved in together. Andy felt so comfortable with Carey that he loosened up a bit on his best behavior and grew a bit careless with his things. He left half-filled coffee mugs on the coffee table, wet towels on the bed, and his shoes at the bottom of the steps. Carey was dismayed to discover these "flaws" and quickly pointed it out to Andy in case he was not aware of how thoughtless he was being.

Andy saw this exchange as the opportunity he had been looking for to let Carey know how much it irritated him when important phone messages were forgotten. He also added that he would appreciate it if the phone line was free, even just ten minutes each night, so he could make a few calls. Though this exchange was not exactly acrimonious, it was a subtle shift from the loving and appreciative place from which they had been operating into pointed observations and mild criticism.

This exchange opened the door for even more critical observations and barbs in the coming weeks. Carey complained more insistently about Andy's habits, resorting to insults. Andy told Carey that he didn't appreciate conversation while he was watching television. They were off and running, and suddenly the spiral of attention noticeably shifted again from observations to more intense criticism.

It was Carey who finally came to see me. Carey was unhappy about their relationship and wanted to find a solution. I explained to her that one person needs to be the one to reverse the focus of attention. I asked if they would both be willing to focus on what they appreciate about the other and stop obsessing about the irritations. I pointed out that willingness is required, and that either one could change the mechanism so that it spiraled upward again by choosing to communicate rather than retaliate. Carey agreed to try.

The next time Andy took an emotional swipe at her, suggesting she had lost one of her business accounts because she was not motivated enough, Carey immediately caught her words before they were spoken, took a deep breath, and called forth the willingness to change the situation. Carey knew that things could not continue the way they were, so she attempted to reverse the negative spiral by shifting from judgment back to acknowledgment.

Carey began by letting Andy know that what he had just said hurt her feelings (shift from judgment to feeling). Then Carey explained that relating in a critical and retaliatory way was not working because the relationship was too precious to both of them and neither of them wanted to hurt the other. By acknowledging the feelings rather than criticizing, Carey was able to disarm Andy and open up a more authentic dialogue about what was going on between them.

GIVE AND TAKE

At the heart of treasuring your loved one lies the energy of giving. Giving is the way you manifest your feelings into tangible form. It is how you extend generosity to your mate, how you reach out with affection, and how you offer your devotion. To give to your partner is to give your love.

WAYS OF GIVING

When most people think of giving, the first thing that comes to mind is presents. From childhood, many people are programmed to believe that love is expressed in pretty packages wrapped up with big bows. Though presents are, of course, important expressions of giving, they are not the only way.

You can give your partner your time, attention, or energy—all gifts that are immeasurably valuable. The greatest gift you can give your partner is something you cannot buy—the gift of yourself. Volunteering to help her with her errands if her day gets over-loaded, or offering to go with her to a dentist appointment she is fearful of are precious acts of giving that can make her feel truly loved. Recently, my friend Debra's boyfriend, Steven, offered to watch her dog for an entire weekend so she could work uninter-rupted on an important project. It was an act of giving that meant more to her than any flowers, chocolate, or jewelry. Simply because you cannot put a dollar value on something does not mean its worth is diminished. Rather, it is those things that are uncountable that are deemed priceless.

Granting wishes is one of the sweetest ways of giving to your partner. Turning your partner's wishes into reality invites a sense of the miraculous into your union. Ask questions related to your love's wishes, dreams, and goals. Regardless of the size of your budget, there are always ways to make wishes come true. If he says he dreams of going to Africa, perhaps a video or a collage of *National Geographic* photographs would bring a smile to his face. If he longs for a vacation, perhaps a mini-holiday in the form of a trip to a day spa or a long, relaxing lunch would suffice for the moment. The key is to listen carefully to what your partner is wishing for and finding creative ways to bestow it.

Finally, giving can come in the form of simple acts of nurturing. Giving your partner a foot or shoulder massage when she is tense, asking how her day was and really listening to the answer, bringing her chicken soup when she is sick, holding her hand when she is frightened, and being with her in her grief are all small acts of giving that can make the difference between a working relationship and a thriving one. Remember, when you share joy with someone, you double it, and when you share grief, you halve it.

RECIPROCITY

The last bite of pie must go to someone. If the two of you are eyeing the last bite and thinking that you should grab it first, you are both assuming that your partner is not thinking of your needs and wants, but rather of his own. You are both locked in "take" mode. If, however, both of you are thinking of the other person, then you will both offer it to the other person—an expression from both people of "give" mode. Perhaps one will accept, or you will split the last bite in half so you can both have one last taste. What really matters is the spirit in which you approach each situation, allowing each person to feel as if he gets his fair share of last bites along the way.

A cycle of reciprocity exists between partners. Ideally, that cycle is balanced and flows easily, and both people feel loved, heard, cherished, respected, and attended to equally. The exchange of give and take is even.

When that cycle is interrupted and the flow of give and take becomes unbalanced, one or both partners will begin to feel cheated and resentful. One ceases to give as much as before, and the other responds by pulling back as well. Suddenly, the partnership is less about give and take and more about take and take. With two people taking and no one giving, the well of love can run dry rather quickly.

When the balance of reciprocity is off, invisible balance sheets appear in each person's unconscious. Each person begins keeping track of who does what, who gives what to whom, and who owes whom favors, time, attention, affection, or whatever else is out of kilter. If the situation escalates and is not addressed, it becomes exacerbated with every exchange and irritation builds. Irritation grows into resentment, and resentments, as we know, create problems.

The key to avoiding this scenario is to notice when the give/get ratio is out of balance and to address and adjust it immediately. This can be done through clear communication and negotiation, so that each person can once again feel of equal importance.

HOW RECIPROCITY IS THREATENED

There are four ways that the cycle of give and take can become imbalanced:

1. When one person gives too little.
2. When one person takes too much.
3. When one person takes too little.
4. When one person gives too much.

The most common complaint stems from the first dynamic—when one person gives too little. Very often, one person has expectations that are not being met, and he will feel some resentment toward his partner for not giving him what he needs or wants. He may end up feeling cheated or taken for granted, and then ill will forms. If your partner is, in your perception, giving too little, you will need to address the situation directly and negotiate a new win-win outcome that reinstates the balance.

This is one of those scenarios where the steps for effective communication (Rule Five) can be very useful. You will need to begin by understanding what it is exactly that you want from your partner. Simply saying that you want "more" is not specific enough; you will need to explain to her clearly what it is that you want "more" of. If your partner is not providing you with what you want or need right now, it is probably because she does not know either what it is or how to give it to you. The more you can help her learn about you and how to give you what you want or need, the happier you both will be.

Right behind, and usually in tandem with, under-giving is over-taking. Those who take more than their fair share deplete their partners and generally further upset the give/take level by not offering their own resources to refill their mate. If your partner takes too much from you without giving in return, resentments will accumulate on your internal balance sheet. You will need to address and adjust these before they become greater than your tolerance can handle.

It is also possible for someone to upset the reciprocity balance by giving too much or taking too little. Many fall into this trap because it seems like the more unselfish way to be. The word "take" has come to seem like a negative, as though it connotes greed. However, what it really means in relationships is openly receiving that which your partner has to offer you.

An imbalance can occur if one partner refuses to move out of the giving role into the receiving role. Such people may say they are doing so out of love or generosity, which indeed they most likely are. Yet the effect of their actions is not necessarily positive. By resisting receiving, they are blocking the natural flow of give and take, upsetting those invisible balance sheets in both partners' minds.

For example, Daniel lavished his partner, Lynn, with expensive gifts and extraordinarily generous offers of assistance. He took her shopping and bought her designer clothing, and he did lovely things like having her car serviced. When Lynn offered gifts—material or immaterial—in return, Daniel charmingly refused, claiming that the only gift he wanted was for her to be happy.

Lynn didn't feel happy, however; what she felt more than anything was guilty. She could not help keeping track of all he was doing for her and thought that he was perhaps doing the same thing, consciously or not. By refusing her offerings, Daniel was creating an imbalance; the flow of give and take was interrupted. Daniel was also denying Lynn the joy that giving to her beloved would bring her.

Over-giving and under-taking are no less a detriment to the balance of your relationship than over-taking or under-giving. Either way, the equilibrium is off center. The only surefire way to maintain the flow of give and take is to give to your partner from your heart, without an agenda, and allow your partner to do the same in return. There are no bonus points for giving more or taking less; the only bonus comes when you both feel equally acknowledged, prioritized, and treasured.

KINDNESS AS A WAY OF LIFE

In the grammar school I went to, report cards had an item entitled "Concern for Others." At that age I could not imagine why being concerned about anyone other than myself was valuable or worthy of high marks. It seemed right that I should only be interested in how I felt, what book I wanted to read, or which toys I got to play with. Being totally self-concerned seemed acceptable to me.

As an adult I realize the importance of concern for others, but now I call it "kindness." I think I really learned about kindness when I became a mother. My self-concern was displaced by a deep concern for my child. I hold her in my consciousness at all times. Even when I am not doing something directly with or for her, she is in my subconscious thoughts. From the moment she was born, her welfare has been my primary interest.

Kindness is the highest and purest form of care giving. It has a specific type of energy that, like a guardian angel, oversees the well-being of another. Kindness has a spirit that is generous, gracious, and knows no bounds. It is selfless, concerned, and committed without being intrusive or oppressive. At its most basic, kindness is simply the act of opening your heart and being genuinely *good* to someone else.

THOUGHTFULNESS IN DAILY LIFE

Thoughtfulness is showing your partner that you care, that he matters, and that you hold him in your consciousness. It means consciously and deliberately doing things to show your love. It is the act of predicting what your partner might like, want, or need, and then going beyond your normal routine to provide it for him.

Thoughtfulness shows up most often in the little things. You have heard the saying "It's the little things that count," and they do. Life is mostly a series of small details strung together; when you take the time and effort to make some of those details sweeter for your partner, you are nourishing him in a way that makes his life better simply because you are in it, and you show you care.

It is easy to find ways to be thoughtful. Do little things without being asked. Have a clean towel ready for your partner when she steps out of the shower, take his favorite shirt to the tailor to get the missing button sewn back on, or pick up her favorite scented soap when it runs out. These small deeds tell your partner that he is a priority and his well-being and happiness matter to you.

For example, when Donna was in a melancholy mood one rainy Sunday, Matt went out and rented some favorite old movies for them to watch. This simple action touched her heart, connected them both, and brightened the evening.

Thoughtfulness does not always have to be romantic, but it can be if the spirit moves you. I was recently on a business trip and needed my husband to send me via overnight mail some extra computer cords. He did, and in the package I found a handwritten note saying, "I miss you, I am thinking of you, and I can't wait to see you when you get home." It was good of him to send the cords, but including that note made the package really special for me.

Try putting Post-it notes on the bathroom mirror expressing your caring: "That's the face I love." "You mean so much to me." "You are so sexy to me!" You can put little notes in unlikely places—the sock drawer, a coat pocket, in the refrigerator. The notes are meant to bring a smile or a laugh of recognition, and to open your partner's heart and touch a cord of specialness.

Sometimes thoughtfulness can be appreciated best when done in secret—I call it "elfism." Elfism is when, like the fairy tale elves, you delight in doing secret good deeds for others and bringing them joy without seeking any notice in return. When you act as an elf toward your beloved, you look for opportunities to do covert things to make her smile, laugh, or twinkle. For example, you might renew her subscription to her favorite magazine, or put change in her expired parking meter.

Thoughtfulness is not a gene that some are born with and some are not. While some people might be more predisposed to it than others, anyone can learn to be thoughtful. All it requires is awareness, a willingness to make your beloved happy, and a little creativity.

RESPECT FOR YOUR PARTNER

Respect means to honor or to hold another in high regard. If you honor your partner, you value his point of view; you listen to his words; you consider his feelings. You treat your love with dignity.

Respect for your partner is what will hopefully prevent you from taking your frustrations or other negative personal feelings out on her. Your partner is your beloved, not your punching bag. While she can certainly provide nurturing and support and be there for you when you need to vent feelings, her purpose is *not* to bear the brunt of those feelings. Coming home and barking at your partner after a hard day displays a lack of respect for her on your part. Remember your partner is your ally, not your opponent, and treat her accordingly.

How you speak to your partner is a reflection of your respect for him. You would not speak to anyone else you held in high regard with sarcasm or put-downs, because that would be inappropriate. Speaking sharply can hurt your partner worse than a physical wound. Take care to listen to the tone of your voice as you speak to your beloved, as he deserves to be addressed with the same regard you would reserve for anyone else you hold in high esteem.

How you treat your partner in the presence of others is another reflection of your respect. If you hold people in high regard, you would not even consider diminishing them. You would not correct or admonish them in front of others, nor would you interrupt them as they speak, as that would signal that you are uninterested in what they have to say.

I went to dinner not too long ago with another couple and was shocked to see the man cutting his wife off every time she tried to make a point. Each time he did, I could see her grow smaller. Clearly he had no respect for her thoughts or opinions.

When you and your partner venture out into the world together, it is each of your responsibilities to be the other's best ambassador. For example, when David accompanies Lane to a business function, he takes great pains to make a good impression on Lane's behalf. Since he respects Lane, he makes sure that his behavior is that of ally and supporter.

Showing respect requires giving your partner the benefit of the doubt in case there is ever a question about his actions or motives. Jumping to accusatory conclusions indicates a lack of trust, and trust goes hand in hand with respect. Respect means you have faith that your partner is innocent until proven guilty and that you stand by him through the process of proving that.

Respect calls forth each partner's best self. Both feel upheld by their partner's high regard, which in turn inspires each to behave accordingly. When two people respect one another, their individual sense of self-worth is increased and their union is nourished as a result.

How you treat your beloved and how your loved one treats you ultimately determines the quality of your relationship. The attention you give one another, the flow of give and take, and the kindness you bestow upon each other are all ways you can treasure your partner and tend to the health and well-being of your union. Take care of your relationship and of your companion, for like a beautiful garden, they are wondrous miracles that require your time, love, attention, energy, and effort to thrive.

RENEWAL IS THE KEY TO LONGEVITY

♥

*Happily ever after means the ability to keep the relationship
fresh and vital.*

For centuries, humankind has searched for the key to immortality. We have circled the globe seeking the fountain of youth and invented countless lotions, potions, and notions, yet eternal life still eludes us.

Meanwhile, our silent fellow tenants on this earth from prehistoric times—the giant sea turtles—have quietly been regenerating and renewing themselves for thousands of years. If one loses a leg, the leg grows back. If they damage their protective shells, the shell repairs itself. The turtles live on and on this way, appearing only to perish at the hands of predators. They have discovered that the secret of longevity is renewal.

So it is with love. The real secret to making your relationship last is having the ability to renew your love and to keep the partnership fresh and dynamic. If part of your relationship is lost, you must regenerate it. If a part gets damaged, you must repair it. When you are able to instill new life into your relationship again and again, you discover the secret to living happily ever after.

KEEPING IT FRESH

One of the most commonly asked questions in long-term relationships is "What happened to the magic?" The initial sparkle of love can lose some of its luster as time goes by, and partners may find themselves wistfully longing for the days when their attraction was intense, their connection clear, and their combined enthusiasm for the union vital. Couples wonder what it would take to imbue their relationship with the same energy, spark, and excitement that fueled it in the beginning. The answer is really quite simple: a relationship requires constant infusion of new and fresh energy. How? Through spontaneous acts, remembering to laugh, reinventing your shared life, and embarking on new journeys of cocreation.

SPONTANEITY

Spontaneity is the essential element of aliveness. By definition, it is unpredictable, uncontrollable, and surprising. Routines become predictable and familiar; to keep a relationship stimulating, you need playfulness, fun, creativity, and surprise.

Think about the moments in your life that were spontaneous. What happened? The analytical, reasonable, logical part was suspended, and you did something impulsive, silly, crazy, even foolish, but it felt wonderful. In relationships, that feeling of wonder can go a long way toward shaking your partnership out of slumber.

A few years ago, my husband said to me, "This Friday you and I are going away somewhere. Be ready at the front door at 4:00 P.M. I will take care of packing whatever you need; your only job is to show up on time." I hardly knew what to think. It wasn't my birthday, Christmas, or Valentine's Day. It wasn't a national holiday or a three-day weekend, and as far as I knew, we weren't celebrating anything. He refused to tell me any more, so I spent the rest of the week wondering about the destination, the logistics, the climate; I wondered whether he could really pack for me. By midweek, I was tingling with excitement and suspense.

On Friday, I was ready at the front door, on time. We got into the car and drove to Burbank Airport. As he ushered me toward the gate marked Las Vegas, I knew: he had planned a weekend getaway in the city of lights! After we checked into our hotel, he walked me blindfolded through the lobby. He led me to the showroom, where we had front row seats to see my favorite comedienne. That was one of the most fun and surprising memories he ever created for me. Thinking of it still makes me feel special and brings a smile to my face.

Spontaneity can come in many forms. It can come as a magical surprise from one of the partners, as mine did, or it can come from a joint decision to just get up and *do something.* The act can be as simple as the two of you walking through a park and suddenly deciding to ride the carousel, or getting dressed up and going dancing, or jumping in the car for a drive in the country. The size and scope of the action is not important. What matters is that you allow yourself to be jolted out of your routine and seize the moment to have fun together. After all, fun is what keeps relationships exciting.

LAUGHTER

Laughter is one of the purest joys in life and one of the happiest things you can enjoy together. It can uplift your spirit, lighten your mood, and warm your heart. When two people share the gift of laughter, they celebrate the wonder and joy of being alive. Their spirits link as they enjoy life through laughter. Remembering to laugh together boosts the joyful spirit that connected you in the first place. Search for the humor in everyday life as often as you can. Keep your ears and hearts open to catch the funny moments or revisit activities or memories that you laughed about together in the past. I know a couple who love Three Stooges movies. Whenever they feel like they need a lift, they rent one and spend the evening giggling next to each other. Another couple, Pam and Louis, end up laughing whenever they go rollerblading, since Louis is far from graceful on skates. When they do this, they keep their relationship sparkling and alive. As you and your mate travel the bumpy road of life together, those moments when you share a smile and feel the tremors of laughter deep in your being keep you in touch with the source of your happiness and increase your relationship's vitality.

Very often, when people search for their ideal mates, a sense of humor is high on their list of must have's. This is because there is something special about being able to laugh together. When you and your partner find the same things funny, you align the childlike parts of yourselves. The delight you felt in the beginning, when you and your partner laughed at the same line in the movie or found the same silly joke hilarious, can be revisited each time you laugh together now. The action will refresh and renew you, again and again.

REINVENTING YOUR REALITY

Marty and Ronnie once told me their life design. He is a dentist and she is a consultant. Every ten years, they take a year off and create an adventure. They end responsibilities in year nine, delegate to competent partners all their patients and clients, and set off for a one-year adventure. To keep their relationship energetic, they reinvent their reality every ten years.

We spend so much time building comfortable lives, that it seems unfathomable to think of changing everything once we are all set. But moving the pieces around is what keeps you and your partner excited about your choices and living in a delighted state of invention and reinvention.

Shifting Circumstances

Hal and Myra had been living in Boston since they were married 34 years ago. Hal was comfortable in his semiretired position as a management consultant, and Myra had been running a local day-care center for years. They were floating along, not necessarily disconnected from one another but not entirely excited about their marriage, either. Everything was, as they both described it with a shrug, "fine."

It was Myra who first had the thought of changing their lives to reinvent their marriage. She recalled that the happiest time for them had been when they first moved to Boston—a new city for both of them. They set up their home, met new friends, and basically assembled a new life together. She figured that if it worked for them once, why not a second time? Since their children were all grown and living elsewhere, she approached Hal with the idea of selling their home and moving to Arizona. They had both loved their vacation there, and since Hal could ostensibly do his job anywhere, there were no restrictions on how far they could move.

Hal was resistant at first. He was comfortable where he was, and claimed that he was "too old" to start over. Myra persisted, and eventually Hal began to her point of view. They had been living the same life for so many years that he could no longer feel anything but just "fine" about it. Since he was only 55, he figured he had at least 30 more years to live, and he certainly did not want to simply live a life that was only "fine" for those 30 years. He agreed to move.

Hal and Myra were like kids again. They delighted in cleaning out their house and fell in love all over again as they sorted through years of stored memories and possessions. They packed up their car and drove across the country to their new home, stopping along the way at various landmarks that they had never seen. When they arrived in Arizona and saw their new, empty home waiting for them to create new memories in, they knew that they had made the right choice.

Sometimes you need to shake things up to keep them stimulating. If picking up and moving is too drastic, there are plenty of other ways to reinvent your life together. Take exotic cooking classes together or make an effort to socialize with new people. Join a new gym and start working out together. Rearrange the furniture in your house, perhaps throwing out what is old and broken, and make an adventure out of finding new pieces to accent your life. Change your daily routine: if you normally drive to work in separate cars, leave a little extra time in the morning so that you can commute together. Take a trip, even if you think you can't, to somewhere you have always wanted to go. Switch roles and responsibilities for a week. Try anything and everything; there are no boundaries when it comes to reinventing the dynamic and breathing new life into your relationship.

COCREATION

Cocreation happens when two people use their creativity, their energy, and their enthusiasm to bring something new into existence. It doesn't really matter what they cocreate; what matters is that they create something that externalizes the bond that has been fused between them. The creation might be a child, a business, a home, a garden, an event, a new vehicle, a craft, a trip—anything that encourages them to pool their energy and their resources together to establish a specific outcome.

Cocreation is the ultimate expression of commitment, as the new entities that are created help build your shared future. For longevity, it is not enough for two people to just touch the edges of their lives together. For example, Gillian and Marcus lived in separate houses and drove their own vehicles that they chose themselves. While each was interested in the other person's personal projects, neither took an active role in forging new "we" projects. While this may be a perfectly legitimate and satisfying way for them to live, they are cutting down on their chances for longevity by neglecting to make any investments in their collective future.

On the other hand, when Katherine and Bernard moved in together, they consciously made the decision to create a home together rather than simply cohabiting. The action of setting up their joint household brought them together as they learned to cooperate, negotiate, and establish an outward expression of who they are as a couple. Their home became a "we" project and is now a shared symbol of the new life they have created together. While their domicile certainly does not guarantee that they will remain together, it does reinforce their ties by keeping their "we" in action.

Throughout the course of any relationship, it will be necessary for you and your partner to join forces in forming and achieving collective goals in order to build a life together. In many long-term relationships, couples work together to create some or all of the basics: a home, children, a joint financial portfolio. These projects externalize—and even symbolize—the connection between them. *Continuing* to create in tandem beyond these basics is what will keep your relationship thriving.

The actual process of creating revitalizes the soul. It nudges the imagination and invites the spirit of aliveness to course through your being. It can awaken the magical parts of you and expand your boundaries of what you can do. What better way to experience that miraculous process than with your beloved?

Plant a garden together. Get a puppy. Share the research and buy a car together. Build a house. Plan a trip. Whatever it is that you choose to create together, the investment of time and energy will go a long way toward reminding you of your soul-to-soul connection and rejuvenating your relationship.

THE SIZZLE FACTOR

The moment you connect with your beloved, a rush of adrenaline courses through your bloodstream. The electricity that ignites the sparks between two people is what I call "the sizzle factor." Sizzle happens when the chemistry between you makes your heartbeat accelerate, your blood flow increase, and your body receptors go on ready alert. The feeling of intense aliveness and vitality is called infatuation, attraction, and passion. The feeling is magnetic and hypnotic and can be as addictive as the most potent drug.

When a couple have been together for many years, the sizzle can wear off. Familiarity, predictability, and routine may create a feeling of stability, security, and permanence, but they do not ignite the sparks. As time passes, you may view your mate as being as familiar and comfortable as your old jeans, and rarely do old jeans inspire passion. So what do you do when the sizzle seems to have faded?

IN SEARCH OF SIZZLE

Some people say, "When you're hot, you're hot; when you're not, you're not." They buy into the fatalistic idea that you can do nothing about it, and that puts the sizzle factor into the hands of chance. However, simply because the sparks may have dimmed does not mean they are extinguished. What these fatalists overlook is that sizzle is an internal temperature that rises from within—not from somewhere outside of you. Your partner and you are responsible for relighting that spark.

Perhaps you have settled into a groove and have become comfortable in your routine. Maybe you and your partner haven't made the effort to get dressed up in a long time, or perhaps careers and the daily grind have become all-consuming lately. It is so easy to get lulled into complacency and not bother to put forth the necessary effort to keep the zest for each other alive.

Sizzle does not arise and then just sustain itself. If you have ever lighted a campfire, you know that it starts with kindling and one spark that catches. After the fire has taken hold, you must add larger sticks and logs to ensure that it grows. When the fire starts to die out, you must fan the embers to reignite the flame. When you fan the embers you add oxygen, which is critical to keep the fire burning. Rekindling sizzle is like breathing new life into a relationship; the oxygen is the effort you put forth to keep it going.

Sizzle rarely extinguishes in an instant. Rather, it is like a slow fade, a subtle erosion of the physical desire that electrified your relationship. This subtle erosion usually saps the sexual energy, and couples can end up going weeks, months, and even years without sharing a passionate moment. When the sex fades, the physical part of your connection is removed, and some partners may be susceptible to turning outside the relationship for gratification. Affairs happen because one or both people stop paying attention and putting forth the energy to keep the sparks alive. If no one fans the flame, it is sure to die out.

REKINDLING THE FLAME

Reigniting the spark once the fire has gone cold may not be easy, but it is not impossible. If your relationship needs some serious sizzle, the first thing you will need to ask yourself is if you are willing to wrest the responsibility out of the hands of fate and do whatever it takes to bring back the magic. Perhaps the hardest part of this process is working up the effort to shake your relationship out of its malaise. It can be tempting to remain cocooned in your present reality. However, if you are feeling the pull of distant memories of your passion, or the stirrings of longing, or sense that you *want* to reignite the spark, then you are halfway out of the cocoon and on your way toward action.

The first step is for you to go back in your mind to the moment that things turned. When was the last point at which you recall the sizzle being alive between you and your mate? You will need to physically, mentally, and emotionally reexperience the sweetness of that memory and relive those feelings of passion in your mind, so that you can reawaken the sizzle *within you.* Connect with your inner memory of the magic and let it enthrall you as it did long ago. That original spark has not been snuffed out; it is only lying dormant, waiting for you to rouse it from its slumber.

When the sizzle is awakened in you, you can then awaken it in the relationship. Holding the sweetness of the past memory in your mind, you will need to bridge the gap between that and the present reality. Yes, but *how,* you might ask? How can you close that chasm? By allowing the renewed glow within you to shine upon your partner, thus relighting the dimmed glow within him.

Start with tiny first steps and inch your way back toward your partner. Perhaps you might start by asking your partner out on an official date—with wine, candlelight, and ambiance—or by suggesting that you do an activity that you both enjoy. You can rent a romantic video, offer to give your partner an unexpected massage, or simply take extra care to look and smell delectable for your partner. By making a gesture toward your beloved, you give him permission to meet you halfway.

If your partner does not respond at first, do not be concerned; you may have simply taken him by surprise. It may take some time, but what was there once will be there again if you persist in your efforts to reignite it. If a campfire is extinguished, do you throw up your hands and say, "It's gone out, it's no use, we might as well forget it"? Not if you want to keep warm! You gather twigs and new logs, starting the process all over again until the flame roars again.

Bringing Back the Magic

After eight years together, Emma and Tim had settled into a comfortable routine. She went to work five days a week, he worked from home in the mornings and tended to their two children in the afternoon. They took turns preparing dinner and spent their evenings with the children, playing games, reading stories, or watching movies. By the time they put the kids to bed, they were both exhausted and fell asleep without spending any time catching up with each other.

The weekends were reserved for errands, Tim's golf game, Emma's gardening, and shuffling the kids between their various activities. When Emma and Tim did get time alone on a Saturday night, they would spend it together, yet apart—she on her end of the couch reading a magazine or talking on the phone, and he on his end engrossed in the television. They were, by their own accounts, happy, though Emma was vaguely aware that a vital part of their relationship had gotten buried amidst the business of their daily lives.

One evening, as she was preparing dinner, she glanced across the table and looked at Tim—really *looked* at him, as though it were the first time she had laid eyes on him. She suddenly recalled how she had felt in the early days of their marriage, when they used to go ballroom dancing on the top of a beautiful hotel. She recalled how delicious Tim smelled as he pulled her close to him, and how thrilling it had felt to be wrapped in his arms, swaying to the music and moving their bodies in rhythm. At that moment, her youngest child spilled her juice all over the dinner table, and Emma was jolted out of her reverie. Yet a remnant of that resurfaced memory remained, and Emma smiled to herself as she formulated her plan.

The following day, with that memory still twinkling in her mind, Emma approached Tim and asked him if perhaps he wanted to hire a baby-sitter for that Saturday night and go dancing. Tim was taken aback at first, and quickly offered several reasons why that would be impossible. There was a game on TV that he wanted to watch, baby-sitters were expensive, and he needed to be up early on Sunday morning. But Emma persisted gently, reminding Tim how long it had been since they had done anything special together. Tim looked at his wife and saw the glimmer in her eye; he realized what Emma was trying to do and he smiled as he said, "Sure, honey."

Emma and Tim got dressed up and went dancing. It had been quite a while since they had really been out on a date with each other, but the sparks began to fly again the moment they stepped on the dance floor. As they looked into each other's eyes, they both knew the magic was back.

HEALING HURTS

There will be times when your partner disappoints you, lets you down, hurts your feelings, or betrays your trust. What then? How can you reconnect when your heart and soul feel bruised or torn by the very person who promised never to bring you harm?

Those are times that you will be called to heal and find the courage and trust to reconnect, renew, and start over. The key to renewal is the ability to forgive, release, and start over again and again. This can be one of the most challenging tasks you will face during the course of your relationship, yet it is also among the most necessary if you are to continue on as an authentic couple.

MENDING WOUNDS YOU HAVE CAUSED

Even in the best of relationships, misunderstandings arise and feelings get inevitably hurt. Disappointments, unfulfilled expectations, broken agreements, and missed commitments happen in life, and although they are usually unintentional, the results are no less painful. When damaged interpersonal tissue is in need of repair, the process must start with a genuine concern for the hurt partner's feelings.

We aspire to be our best selves with our partner, and when we fall short of the mark—which as humans we invariably do from time to time—it is a disappointment. How you deal with the hurt feelings you caused, inadvertently or not, is one of the keys to maintaining the authenticity within your relationship.

The best thing you can do for your partner in this situation is to take responsibility for your actions. When you refuse to own up to your part in hurting your partner's feelings or injuring her pride, you add insult to injury by not giving her the respect she deserves.

Francis and Katie were out to dinner with a few friends when the subject of cooking came up. Katie had always been self-conscious about her weight, so she usually tried to cook healthy, low-fat meals. The mood at dinner was jovial, and Francis did not realize that he was being hurtful when he made a joke about not getting fed any gourmet meals until Katie finally loses those ten pounds. "Which means," he said, winking, "I won't be enjoying any fancy dinners anytime soon."

Katie was embarrassed, as were the rest of the people at the table. Francis had taken the joke too far and hurt Katie's feelings. On the way home that night, Katie confronted Francis. Francis immediately grew defensive, and rather than owning up to the damage he might have caused his beloved's self-esteem, he responded that she always took things he said too seriously. Katie was further upset that Francis could not at least admit to and apologize for the fact that he had done something that hurt her.

Beyond taking responsibility for any damage you have caused, the second best thing you can offer your beloved is a sincere apology, from the heart, along with a well-thought-out explanation for why you did what you did. When spoken truthfully, the words "I'm sorry" can go a long way toward mending wounded feelings.

Do not say these words if you do not mean them! You will only cause your partner worse pain by issuing hollow sentiments. "I'm sorry" means that you truly regret what you have done and would not do it again given the same opportunity. If you do not feel this way, then rather than offering false platitudes, use your communication skills to offer your perspective and work through the impasse. Your partner will appreciate your candor more than an insincere apology.

FORGIVENESS

It has been said that "to err is human, to forgive divine." The act of forgiveness requires that you rise above your negative human feelings and release them in order to find your way back to the spiritual source of your being. No easy task, of course, but a very necessary one in the arena of love.

There will be times when you or your partner do something that angers or hurts the other; you are both human, and as humans we all have lessons to learn. Whether an inconsiderate action, a broken agreement, or a violation of your shared ethics, how you choose to handle it will determine whether your relationship continues on its authentic course or veers off track. At those moments you will be faced with a choice: keep the negative feelings by holding a grudge, thereby driving a wedge between you and your partner, or release them through forgiveness. Forgiveness is what reconnects you and allows your relationship to regenerate again and again. Forgiving your significant other repairs the rift between you and keeps your relationship intact.

A wound inflicted in the context of a love relationship is one of the most painful. The very nature of love relationships is based on the partners' ability to rely on one another and to behave in respectful, loving ways. The emotions that underlie your union will make any hurt feel more intense and any wound harder to heal.

The forgiveness process has two prongs: the thoughts that come up in response to the offense, and the feelings. The thoughts and feelings are interwoven; they are linked together in a spiraling dance of realization and reaction. Your thoughts are evaluative and they conceptualize the situation into manageable pieces. They are what echo in your mind as you wonder if your partner is still worth the effort or decide that what has happened is unfair and out of the realm of what you bargained for.

Feelings, on the other hand, have no words for them. They are the intangible, raw emotions that arise in response to your thoughts. You may feel angry, resentful, betrayed, or emotionally abandoned. Feelings are the nonrational, gut reactions that radiate out from your emotional core.

The thought process is the way you run facts through your mind and attempt to understand what motivated your partner to act that way. You may need to ask your partner to explain his reality to you so that you can make sense of his actions. Minds, before fully forgiving, search for ongoing evidence that the wrong will not be repeated. When your mind is convinced that your partner will not repeat his transgression, then you are halfway there.

Mental forgiveness involves a weighing process. You will need to assess in your mind whether it is worth continuing to expend energy by holding a grudge or whether you and your partner would be better served if you released it. You will need to weigh the satisfaction of being righteous against the burden of holding on to your anger. When you decide that carrying your grudge and punishing your partner is no longer worth your valuable time and energy, you will then be able to fully release the issue from your mind.

The feelings that arise when you are called to forgive more major transgressions are a bit more difficult to work through, since feelings are not linear or logical. If you are feeling disappointed, let down, or hurt, then you must process these emotions by fully experiencing, expressing, and then releasing them in order to truly heal. By venting your feelings, you can process the transgression and let it work its way out of your system. The more severe the wrongdoing, the longer the time required for healing.

Ultimately, forgiveness comes when you are able to shift your perception and view your partner as a human who has weaknesses that need to be forgiven, just as you would ask for your errors to be. Making this inner shift is what moves you into the realm of the divine.

Forgiveness is not easy. The old adage "time heals all wounds" is true, but healing also requires that you do your own internal work as well. Whether the transgression is minor or major, time alone will not repair the fracture unless you actively work to release any pain or anger.

A SMALL LESSON IN FORGIVENESS:
STU AND AMELIA

Stu was having a great day. He was in the flow of his work and getting into the rhythm of the contract he was drafting when Amelia called. She, on the other hand, was having a frustrating day and started taking her feelings out on him. She picked a fight over something insignificant, and suddenly Stu's "up" bubble was burst and his day was no longer cruising along as it had been before she called.

Stu hung up the phone angry with Amelia for bringing him down, especially since she knew he had been going through a difficult time the past few weeks and desperately needed to get his rhythm back. He was annoyed that she had been so insensitive to his needs, and he let her know his thoughts later that evening. They argued a bit, and Amelia finally apologized sincerely and assured Stu she did not mean to ruin his day.

In order for Stu to shift from anger into forgiveness, he needed to understand why Amelia had acted as she had. She explained to him that she just was not thinking when she made that call, and promised him that she would be more considerate the next time she called him at work with anything negative. When he put himself into Amelia's reality by imagining how she came to behave as she did, he understood that the issue was minor and that she had not intended to cause him any unhappiness. He was then able to release it by mentally declaring it "no big deal." He forgave Amelia immediately and they moved on.

A BIG LESSON IN FORGIVENESS:
WALLY AND AMBER

Wally, a stand-up comic by trade, was always the life of the party. Everyone loved him for his hilarious sense of humor. Amber was quiet and more introspective than Wally. Despite their obvious personality differences, Wally was drawn to Amber's mysterious nature, and Amber enjoyed Wally's ability to make her laugh. They clicked almost immediately, and their relationship developed into a deep and meaningful partnership.

One evening, when Amber and Wally were at a party, Amber was getting a drink when, out of the corner of her eye, she saw a voluptuous redhead throw her arms around Wally and nuzzle up to him. As she watched from across the room, she noticed that he seemed to know her and was not resisting her advances. Amber was shocked at first and then sickened as she realized what this might mean. Not wanting to cause a scene, she quietly approached Wally and said, "I'm leaving. If you care to join me, now is the moment." Wally, taken by surprise, saw the seriousness of the moment and realized he'd better go with her.

Amber did not speak until they arrived at Wally's house. Then the confrontation began. As it turned out, Wally had met the red-head when he had been on the road. It had seemed harmless enough at the time, and he never felt a need to tell Amber about the encounter because it had only happened once. Amber felt betrayed, deceived, and ejected from the safety of their loving union. She could hardly believe that Wally would behave as he did, and seriously doubted her discernment ability. She had always thought of Wally as not the type to wander, and this sudden turn of events left her mind reeling.

Wally apologized profusely, promising to make it up to her any way he could. He assured her that it was she whom he loved, and that he was so remorseful for how this had made her feel that he would never do such a thing again. He spent the next few weeks going out of his way to demonstrate to Amber how precious she was to him and how truly sorry he was for what he had done.

The ball was in Amber's court. In order to forgive Wally, she needed to be with all the pain and tears until the process was complete. She allowed herself to fully experience and express all the emotions that arose, so they could work their way through and out of her. As needed, she vented, raged, cried, and externalized the feelings any way that she could in order to release them.

Throughout the healing process, Amber also needed to work through her thoughts as well, evaluating whether or not she was even willing to *consider* forgiving Wally. Eventually, her reasoning led her to see that Wally was not a monster, only a man who had taken a wrong turn. She decided that it was worth it for her to stay the course and invest her energy in forgiving Wally rather than holding on to her righteous anger and continuing to punish both of them. She chose forgiveness, although it was not easy; she eventually released her anger and turned back toward Wally so they could reconstruct their relationship in tandem.

REPAIRING BROKEN TRUST

Trust is the foundation of any authentic union. Without trust, your foundation is built on quicksand, and your relationship will quickly sink into the depths below.

When trust has been broken, it needs to be repaired. If too much time goes by without the damage being attended to, the wound will grow more and more insidious. Repairing trust requires deep contrition and advanced levels of forgiveness—neither one is easy. It can be humiliating to be contrite when you have transgressed and seemingly impossible to forgive when you have been betrayed. Albeit advanced lessons, they will be asked of all couples who pursue the path of authenticity. There is no side-stepping.

If your relationship has been challenged because of a breach in your partner's trust, you will need to move beyond sincere apologies into making amends. It will be your responsibility to compensate for your wrongdoing and earn back the trust of your beloved. Making amends requires that you go above and beyond what is usual to prove and demonstrate to your partner that you are willing to do whatever it takes to make up for the damage you have caused.

Bobby could hardly look his wife, Margie, in the eye when he confessed to her that he had gambled away a large portion of their life's savings. She was horrified and felt utterly betrayed by Bobby's lack of concern for their family's financial well-being. Bobby felt terrible, and after owning up to his actions and apologizing from his heart, he set about making amends for what he had done. He sold his beloved antique car and used that money to carefully invest in high-yield mutual funds. He gave up his membership at a local country club, where he went every weekend to play tennis, and instead spent his weekends putting in extra hours at his law firm to earn back the money he had lost. In addition, he also attended Gamblers' Anonymous meetings every Tuesday night.

Eventually, Margie forgave him for what he did. Seeing him put in such effort to make amends reestablished her faith in Bobby's commitment, and she soon joined him in his efforts to create more income for their family using her talent as an artist. When Bobby saw Margie smile and wink at him as she sold her first painting, he was finally able to fully forgive himself, knowing that they were a team once again.

Whichever partner caused the foundation of the relationship to be shaken will be the one ultimately responsible for repairing the damage. If it was you who betrayed your partner's trust, it will also be you who will bear the burden of earning back that trust. Your partner will need to work toward forgiveness, but you will be the one whose actions determine whether your relationship is regenerated or destroyed.

Rebuilding trust is a challenging process that requires time, dedication, and faith. Yet there is no damage that cannot be repaired if both partners are willing to glue back together the shards of their shattered trust and to reopen their hearts to each other.

RITUALS AND CELEBRATIONS: CREATING AND MEMORIALIZING MEMORIES

Ritualizing events means taking yourselves and your precious moments seriously. It means that you are willing to say, "This is a moment we want to honor and to confer special meaning upon." It means you set aside the time, pay the proper attention, and remember that something special is happening. Creating rituals to commemorate your important moments and anniversaries will enable you to build an experiential scrapbook of your relationship that will fortify you and your partner every time you revisit it.

The purpose of wedding ceremonies is to consecrate the bond between two partners and to create a marker that says, "It began here." Each subsequent anniversary will put that couple in touch with the memory of their choice to unite. You and your beloved can employ that dynamic, whether you are wed in marriage or not, by ritualizing and celebrating all your important moments and memories along the way.

Rituals are conducted with intention and attention to detail. A ritual can be a gathering or a party. It can be the breaking of bread, opening of presents, or lighting of special candles. At times it can be more spiritual in nature, as in a religious event or a sacred ceremony. It is up to you and your partner to create the rituals that matter to the two of you.

For example, Jeff and Laura go to the annual film festival where they met to remind them of their first times together. Alison and Matt go skiing every spring because they met in the mountains and it renews their love of nature, exercise, and romantic evenings in the snow. Johnny and Robin go to their favorite sushi restaurant to remember and celebrate meeting in Japan years ago. All three of these couples have found ways to revisit their initial connection and thus to keep their relationship alive.

Time is ephemeral. A moment is here now, and in an instant it has passed. You cannot change the course of time, but you can create memories to last you a lifetime. Live life fully in the present; create your memories and rituals now, so that you will be able to revisit them in the future.

Remember to celebrate. Celebrate the simple things: the fact that you are both alive, that you have found each other, that are you blessed with all that you have. Celebrate each day the miracle of your love, and create small rituals to honor the special love that passes between you: a kiss before drifting off to sleep each night, a special toast you make to each other, a secret code word that means something to only the two of you. Start today, and make every day that you spend together a day to acknowledge your love and renew your commitment.

Happily ever after is not a static state of being. Fairy tales would have us believe that the lovers enter a perpetual state of bliss from the moment they find each other and continuing on forever. I have never seen a fairy tale that discloses the reality of true love—that it requires a constant infusion of fresh energy to sustain itself.

Sadly, so many people toss their relationship away once it loses its initial shine. Yet like a precious antique lamp, it takes only a little polish, some ingenuity, and effort to restore it to its valuable condition. Throwing it away without even attempting to renew it might be a costly mistake. Like that lamp, a relationship's luster will improve with age if you continually give it the care it needs to keep it beautiful. Once you uncover its essential beauty, it becomes a priceless object that will bring you joy for years to come.

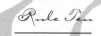

Rule Ten

YOU WILL FORGET ALL THIS THE MOMENT YOU FALL IN LOVE

♥

You know all these rules inherently. The challenge is to remember them when you fall under the enchanting spell of love.

$\mathcal{I}$n Shakespeare's *A Midsummer Night's Dream,* a mischievous fairy dabs the nectar of magic flowers onto the eyes of the humans sleeping in the forest, causing the unsuspecting mortals to fall hopelessly under the spell of love when they awaken. Professions of undying love and foolish demonstrations of devotion follow.

Real life is not so different from life in that imaginary forest. The enchantment that the first blush of love brings can be intoxicating, and our eyes can be sprinkled with stardust that only permits us to see the glorious wonder of our beloved. Our hearts fill with warmth and tenderness as elation courses through our veins. The potency of love fills our being and elevates us to a state of spellbound ecstasy.

Falling in love is like being enveloped in a magical cloud. The air feels fresher, the flowers smell sweeter, food tastes more delectable, and the stars shine more brilliantly in the night sky. You feel light and lofty as though you are floating through life, and your problems and challenges suddenly seem insignificant and easily surmountable. Your body feels alive, your skin tingles, and you awaken in the morning with a smile on your face. You are suspended in a state of supreme delight.

Love is a feeling and an action that arises from the most natural and primal place within us. *Relating,* however, is a process that is learned. This process allows feelings of love to be expressed, cultivated, and sustained. A relationship is the vessel that carries the precious cargo of love through time.

These ten rules, which we already know within us, are the basis of authentic relationships. The real challenge is to remember them in the midst of playing the game of love. If you remember these universal truths, your love will have the greatest opportunity to flourish and your relationship the best potential for success.

TEMPORARY AMNESIA

Up until this point, you may have agreed with these ten rules, but when you fall in love, you forget a great deal that you once knew. Love has a tendency to eclipse most rational, logical, and reasonable thought patterns.

For example, when Olivia met Kevin, she fell head over heels for his boyish charm. He was witty and adoring and lavished her with gifts, beautiful love notes, and unending compliments. The only problem was that Kevin lived in another state, 2,000 miles away from Olivia.

So enraptured was Olivia that despite the protests and warnings of her friends and family, she quit her job, gave up her lease on her apartment, and moved to the city where Kevin lived after knowing him for only three months. They both believed that the strength of their love would compensate for any inconvenience that a major life move would cause. Within a few weeks of her arrival, reality began to creep into the cracks between the love notes and the adoration, and Olivia suddenly awoke from her reverie and realized the enormity what she had done.

THE POWER OF LOVE

Love is a kind of elixir or aphrodisiac that lures us out of reality and into the realm of fantasy. It acts like a drug creating an altered state of consciousness. Many factors contribute to this intoxicating effect. First, it appears as if someone really special deeply cares about you. Your most basic desire to be loved, cherished, and adored is being filled, which can temporarily patch some of the holes in your soul. Second, that same person focuses most if not all of her attention on you, which can be a euphoric feeling. Third, it looks like your dream may yet come true after all; you may be able to live the fairy tale existence of happily ever after. The hope that arises from this belief can be so potent as to blind you to any opposing reality.

Fourth, and perhaps most powerful of all, your hormones get the signal and your body chemistry takes over. When you fall in love, PEA *(phenylethylamine)* is released and creates feelings of euphoria, calmness, and well-being. PEA, coincidentally, is also found in chocolate, which is the reason that chocolate acts like a panacea for many people. PEA coursing through your system can eclipse your sense of reality by making you feel naturally high.

Sexual energy is one of the most potent forces in the universe, and when it has you in its grasp, it can feel as though nothing else matters other than the feel of your beloved's flesh pressed against yours.

The temporary amnesia you experience can cause you to ignore if not forget rational, sound, and sensible data about directing your feelings of love into an authentic relationship. Suddenly, through the haze of infatuation and sexual attraction, you may give in to certain misperceptions. You might even override the notion that you need to love yourself first, thinking instead "My love gives me all the love I could ever need." You will most likely believe that you and your partner are special and different and that you can bypass the steps of exploration, evaluation, and building intimacy. The intensity of your connection may feel so powerful and solid that you believe you can advance directly to commitment. You may be swayed by thoughts like "This must be *it*, if it feels so right," or "This is different—no one has ever experienced this kind of deep connection."

Perhaps you will disregard the importance of communication, believing that you and your partner are so psychically aligned that you will both always just *know* what the other is thinking or feeling. You may believe that negotiation is unnecessary for you and your partner, because agreements happen naturally. You may imagine that nothing in your relationship could ever change, because you are certain that you will always treasure each other as you do now.

All these beliefs seem real in the moment, when you are in the grip of infatuation and passion. Once the patina of perfection wears off, it is important that you recall all the rules for creating authentic relationships. Only through time and experience will you recognize these beliefs as temporary suspensions of reality and be able to strike a balance between losing yourself in the rapture and maintaining your rational mind.

REMEMBERING THE RULES

The feelings that new love brings are to be relished, for they are among the most miraculous pleasures of life. Savor the beginning of your romance, for the special feelings and precious memories created in that time will form a basis for what might later ripen into a lasting union. Treasure and enjoy every sweet moment.

At the same time, your challenge will be to try to remember these ten rules in the midst of your euphoria. Enjoy the experience, but also try, if you can, to keep these rules in the back of your mind so that you can peek through the veil of temporary amnesia before you mistake the initial throes of chemistry or infatuation for true love.

The way out of temporary amnesia is through reminding yourself of everything you already know. Simply because they do not seem applicable or necessary at this moment does not mean their truth is any less valid. If an airplane flies behind a mountain out of view, does that mean it disappears? The airplane exists *even though you cannot see it.* If you cannot see the value of the rules, it just means you are temporarily blinded to them.

The key here is to recognize that what you may be feeling in the heat of love may not necessarily be objective reality. Think of infatuation like a fever: while under its grasp, you may see, hear, or feel things that may seem very real to you but may, in fact, be delusory. It is not until the fever breaks that you can test reality and determine what was real and what was hallucination. Like a fever, you will need for the magic of infatuation to dissipate slightly before you can truly know what is real.

Remind yourself of these rules often, even—and especially—when you think they are irrelevant or inapplicable to your situation. This is the only way to be sure that the relationship you construct to house your love will be an authentic one that can stand the test of time.

RESPONSES TO LOVE

Each person will have his own personal and individual reaction to the potency of love. The "thinkers" may be surprised to see logic and reason drift away as they float through their days on cloud nine. "Feelers" may be so overwhelmed by their emotions that they get a bit wacky. Those with boundary issues may lose their center and have difficulty maintaining their identity in relation to their mate. Still others may burrow themselves so deeply into their new reality that they lose touch with the anchors that once kept them rooted to their life. Love is a powerful force which, like the magical nectar in Shakespeare's play, can bewitch those it touches.

ENTERING DREAMLAND

Love can fuzzy our rational minds in an instant. When faced with the enticement of romance or the excitement of passion some intelligent and seemingly level-headed people lose their grounding. They may suddenly write sonnets or spend their paychecks on expensive gifts for their sweetheart. They stare out the window dreamily, sing love songs out loud that are playing on the radio, and act like goofy, love-struck teenagers. Judicious thought is tossed to the wind as they plunge ahead, driven by their emotions and fueled by chemistry.

This dreamy state can cause them to become absentminded. They focus on fantasies and thoughts of their new love and they cease to pay attention to the details of everyday life. When my friend Kathy fell in love, she went through a stage in which she forgot to turn out lights, lost her car keys, left the bath water running, and forgot to put on the emergency brake. Others have been known to leave the gas on, misplace their wallet, or leave the door ajar.

The beauty of new love is the way it makes you feel. The only caveat is to be sure that you do not lose your head to the point of endangering your well-being or happiness. You will need to keep some semblance of rational behavior to protect yourself from any potential damage, be it physical or emotional. You alone are responsible for your own heart and body, and you will need your head at times to guide you to ensure your overall best interest.

THE OVERWHELM OF EMOTIONS

If your passion rather than your rational mind influences your thoughts and actions, you may find yourself feeling a bit off balance. Some peoples' emotions surge so forcefully that they find themselves doing things that, if they were not spellbound by infatuation, they might have deemed foolish. This is where the phrase "being a fool for love" comes from. In the movie *There's Something About Mary*, the men do crazy things to get close to Mary. One of them goes out of his way to have one of Cameron Diaz' shoes, another pretends he is a pizza delivery man to get in close proximity to her, and still another spies on her to find out the description of her ideal man in order to become her "perfect guy."

If you become fixated on the elixir of love, you may experience manic feelings of craving your beloved's attention up to the point of compulsion. These unstable feelings can arise when your overflowing emotional tank eclipses your sound mind. You feel like you *must* see your new love immediately; you have to inhale his scent, hear the music of his voice, and bask in his presence. The thought of being apart from him even for a brief period is unbearable. Your beloved becomes like an addiction to you.

Falling in love is a mixed bag of gifts and afflictions. Accelerated heartbeat, inability to sleep, difficulty concentrating, preoccupation with each contact with your beloved all sound like a description of sickness rather than bliss. Passion can be sweet one moment and bitter the next, depending on how it is perceived. The intense feelings of longing that love evokes can be both a blessing and a burden.

Throughout the history of time, poets, artists, and songwriters have created masterpieces dedicated to the intensity of this longing. If you find yourself entrenched in it, the best you can do is center yourself, stay connected to the people, places, and rituals that are your personal anchors, and strive to achieve the balance between losing your mind and satisfying your heart.

MAINTAINING YOUR IDENTITY

It is common for people to lose their sense of "I" temporarily when they enter the realm of "we." That is to be expected as you and your beloved cocoon, focusing all your time and attention on becoming enmeshed with each other. Your auras become entangled as do your everyday lives. Your time becomes consumed with activities and commitments with this new person, and the majority of your energy goes toward her. All of this is initially necessary to begin the formation of "we."

The tricky part comes when both people need to regain their sense of "I" in order to continue contributing to the greater "we." The lure of seamless togetherness can become hypnotic, and you may want to remain enmeshed. Yet in order for the greater "we" to continue growing, each person will need to define boundaries and continually strengthen their individual "I."

STAYING CENTERED

Sophia dated three men while she was in college, each one stylistically and characteristically different and each one part of a separate social scene. Jim was a rugby player who spent his free time working out at the gym with his friends. Doug was a preppy, conservative literature major who devoted the majority of his time to his studies. Charlie was a fun-loving guy who tended bar at the campus pub.

With each man, Sophia adopted his style, activities, hobbies, and habits. When she was with Jim, she exercised and hung out at the gym. She wore sweats and started using phrases like "load up on carbs" and "spot me." When she dated Doug, she wore khakis and loafers and spent untold hours at the library. With Charlie, she stayed out all night drinking and dancing. Her own identity metamorphosed each time she dated a new man.

Like a chameleon that blends in with her surrounding environment, Sophia molded herself to the image of each man. She repeatedly shifted her frame of reference so that it was a match with theirs. From the outside, it appeared that Sophia desperately wanted these men to approve of her. While this may have been the case, the underlying cause was Sophie's inability to stay centered in who she was, regardless of whom she was seeing.

Staying centered is what enables you to maintain your identity within the context of a "we" reality. It requires that you remember what it is that makes you uniquely *you* and enables you to stay on course with your own path. It means that you continually ask the question "Who am I in relation to you?" and are clear about the answer. While it will be necessary, and even desirable at times, for you to be flexible, accommodating, and adaptive, it will be your responsibility to make sure not to become overly pliant. The only thing you have to lose by not being vigilant about this is yourself.

SECURING YOUR ANCHORS

Anchors are the people, places, and touchstones that keep you connected to yourself and your life. Anything that brings you back to center, be it a trusted friend or family member, a specific environment, or a certain ritual, is an anchor. Anchors ground you by serving as reminders of who you are, your choices, and your authentic nature.

Imagine if you awakened tomorrow morning stricken with complete memory loss. How would you begin to fill in the missing pieces? How would you recall who you are, what you do, what you like, what you want, and what matters most to you? Most likely you would turn to the anchors in your life—friends, family, memorabilia, old letters, sensory experiences—in the hopes that they could jar a stuck memory or jiggle your consciousness so you recall the facts and data. Perhaps the scent of vanilla would trigger you to recall your home and the feelings of safety that are attached to that sense. Perhaps a photo of you and your spouse would alert the sensors in your brain and bring forth the memory of a cruise you took years ago, or perhaps having a conversation with an old friend would remind you of your genuine priorities.

Staying rooted to your anchors can alleviate the metaphorical amnesia that falling in love causes. If you become disconnected from your core, your anchors will remind you of who you were and what was important to you before you became enmeshed with this new entity. Of course, you will experience growth and change when you merge into a "we." The difference between healthy merging and unhealthy merging, however, is that healthy merging allows you to expand and include your "I" in the greater "we." Unhealthy merging mandates that you disconnect from your life and give up your "I" and all of your familiar anchors entirely.

The Danger of Disconnection

Charlotte was a 40-year-old divorcee living in Idaho. She was independently wealthy, and her family had run successful businesses for generations. She traveled abroad and met a Greek man named Dimitri. Charlotte was swept away by Dimitri's charm, his business acumen, and his worldliness. He became the center of her universe. Dimitri was a very domineering and controlling person, and as the months of their relationship passed, he slowly convinced Charlotte that he knew all the answers and that she should listen to him and only him on all accounts.

Charlotte was so enraptured with Dimitri that she became like a Stepford wife in a movie with the same name, obeying his every wish and command. He told her how to run her business, how to discipline her children, and how to wear her hair, and she eventually only made decisions and took actions with his sanction and agreement. She gave up many of her personal touchstones, including listening to opera (Dimitri did not like music), riding horses (not on Dimitri's list), and lunching with her childhood friends (Dimitri thought that a waste of time). When her friends and family members expressed alarm at her actions and issued warnings that perhaps Dimitri was not necessarily the best partner for her, she brushed them off, saying, "You couldn't possibly understand." She was so enmeshed with Dimitri that his views became unequivocally hers, and she lost touch with what had been important to her prior to him.

Each time someone from her inner circle tried to remind her of the strong-willed, independent Charlotte they once knew, Charlotte told Dimitri. He responded by insisting that her friends and family were only trying to impede her growth and that they were just jealous of her. Eventually, Dimitri convinced Charlotte to disassociate herself from "those influences," and she cut her emotional ties to her anchors.

After Dimitri isolated Charlotte from her friends and family, he then moved to the States and became involved with her family business. Charlotte became pregnant and had their child, starting what she believed would be a happy family. After two years, Dimitri had drained the business of all its assets. He left Charlotte and the baby and returned to Greece.

It took Charlotte a long time to reassemble the pieces of her life. Besides all the financial damage inflicted on her business, she needed to repair the emotional fractures created between her family and friends and her. She needed to forgive herself, restore her sense of confidence in her inner radar, and reinstate her ability to make sound choices. It was not until years later that she was able to reflect and understand what had really happened; then, in hindsight, she was able to distill the lessons from that chapter of her life.

Charlotte's tragic story is unfortunately not unique. There are people in this world, like Dimitri, who appear as the proverbial wolf in sheep's clothing. When you relinquish your inner knowing, your power, your ability to choose, and your anchors, you are asking for trouble. You become susceptible to such people, and the wounds they can inflict can be emotionally deadly. When you ignore and abandon all your anchors, you set yourself adrift on a course without radar, life preservers, or safety mechanisms.

Falling in love can be one of the most thrilling and wondrous experiences of your life. It can also be one of the most challenging, for it is the very act of "falling" that knocks you off balance. Stay connected to your anchors, especially when you're launching into the uncharted waters of a new relationship. Anchors will keep you rooted to what makes you essentially *you*, and that will prevent you from an emotional shipwreck.

them and presented them to you for your happiness and well-being. You already know these rules in the depth of your psyche. The challenge is to remember them when the fairies sprinkle stardust in your eyes and you fall under the enchanted spell of love.

May you love and be loved in the healthiest of relationships for as long as you wish.

REMEMBERING YOUR ESSENCE

The underlying key to maintaining your identity and
track when you fall under the spell of love is to rememb
you learned in Rule One. By remembering your essence ar
uing to honor and love yourself, you give yourself the be
to build an authentic and successful relationship out of th
ble ecstasy that is love.

You must love yourself first. If you feel fully loved by
you will not be tempted to lose yourself in another. If
whole and complete within yourself, then you will main
center. If you feel cared for and honored at your core, the s
be only too clear. If you have clear criteria for how you wa
treated, then you will have a ballast to keep you on course
require respect, kindness, caring, and integrity, then any l
that is other than that will be obvious. If you accept your
who and what you are, then you will recognize anyone who
equally validating. If you have trustworthy anchors surro
you who will tell you the truth, you only have to pay atten
those you love and trust over time. If you are firmly groun
who you are, you will never find yourself in a relationship th
you at risk. Even though you will forget all these rules the m
you fall in love, you can remember them, and awaken from
dreamlike state by remembering who you are.

The rules of authentic relationships have been true since lov
blossomed. They were not created by me; I have just summa

Summary

♥

" 'Tis better to have loved and lost than never to have loved at all."
Alfred Lord Tennyson

In the game of love, I have won and I have lost. I learned how to open up and love again when I thought I never could. I am blessed to have authentic love in my life.

Love, loving, being loved, relating, and authentic relationships were never taught in my home or my school. I learned it from the school of life, the lifeshop. I learned through trial and error—experimenting and growing from the pain of a broken heart and shattered dreams.

I learned to start over, to trust again, to open up; I learned to believe that if I were to model the love I want by loving myself, that the right person, hopefully my soul mate, would show up and be magnetized to me.

Was I lucky, persistent, tenacious, or blessed? Probably all of the above are true. I felt in my heart that I was meant to partner, so I kept interviewing until the right one came along. At the same time, I continued to do my inner work so that when he showed up I would recognize him.

I feel blessed to have manifested Michael, a man who is strong enough to be gentle and gentle enough to be strong. He is willing to lead or follow, work or play, laugh or be serious, share grief or celebrate, and hold my hand throughout the journey.

Loving, losing, learning the lessons, and reloving have been my path. I am pleased to open the door and share it with you. I cannot say the journey has been easy, but it has been worth it.

Thank you for joining me on the path to authentic loving. Love yourself first; learn your love lessons and treasure your partner each precious moment you are fortunate enough to be together.

Chérie Carter-Scott, Ph.D.

About the Author

Dr. Chérie Carter-Scott is a *New York Times* #1 bestselling author, entrepreneur, international lecturer, management consultant, trainer, coach, and seminar leader.

In 1974 Dr. Carter-Scott founded The MMS (Motivation Management Service) Institute, Inc., which specializes in personal growth training programs and workshops for both the corporate and private sectors worldwide. For the past 25 years, she and her business partner and sister, Lynn Stewart, have empowered hundreds of thousands of individuals to redesign their lives personally and/or professionally by way of their unique and inspired work.

The Inner Negotiation Workshop (INW) is the heart of the public workshop series; the INW represents the passion, perhaps even the calling, Chérie and Lynn share for facilitating others in initiating life-changing choices in their lives.

The workshop is designed to facilitate the rules explained in this book, as well as many of the concepts discussed in *If Life Is a Game, These Are the Rules.* This workshop is a human greenhouse in which your authentic self emerges and is given the opportunity to grow. When you are connected to your authentic self, you will be able to envision, articulate, magnetize, and manifest the relationship you have always dreamed of.

You may contact The MMS Institute for information regarding

- Personal Growth Programs or Professional Trainings:
  The Inner Negotiation Workshop
  The Consultants Training (coaching skills)
  Advanced Consultants Training (meditation skills)
  Leadership Training
- Corporate Consultation or Trainings:
  Visioning
  Managing Change in Corporations
  Team Building
- Management Development Courses:
  Communication Skills
  Conflict Management
  Consultive Sales Training
  Customer Satisfaction
  How to Run Successful Meetings
  Interviewing Skills
  Performance Appraisal
  Presentation Skills
  Stress Management
  Time Management
- Other books, tapes, and products by Dr. Chérie Carter-Scott:
  If Life Is a Game, These Are the Rules: Ten Rules for Being Human

Negaholics: How to Overcome Negativity and Turn Your Life Around

The Corporate Negaholic: How to Deal Successfully with Negative Colleagues, Managers, and Corporations

The New Species: The Evolution of the Human Being

The Inner View: A Woman's Daily Journal

Chicken Soup for the Global Soul, coauthored with Jack Canfield and Mark Victor Hansen, scheduled to be published in March 2001

- To be added to The MMS Institute's mailing list or to submit a story to *Chicken Soup for the Global Soul* or booking Dr. Carter-Scott to speak to your group,

  Call: I (800) 321-6342 (NEGA) or

  in California: (805) 563-0789

  visit our Web site: www.ifloveisagame.com

  Fax: (805) 683-0639

  E-mail: info@ifloveisagame.com

Dr. Carter-Scott resides in Nevada with her husband and daughter.

Dear Reader

The world of love may seem attractive, enticing, even seductive. It may, at times, seem unclear, confusing, and worrisome. Why does love seem so easy for some and so difficult for others? How do two compatible people ever find each other? In a fast-paced, demanding, and confusing world, how do you know what is real?

If Love Is a Game, These Are the Rules has been written for you. It presents the ten rules for authentic relationships, the universal principles that govern love relationships. It is to be used as your guide as you navigate through the sea of love. Use it as a reference book as you travel through the various phases. Refer to it when you have questions or if you are confused, uncertain, in doubt, or afraid that you have made the wrong choice.

If the principles in this book resonate with you and you want more morsels of universal wisdom, you are invited to continue your spiritual path through our coaching, workshops, trainings, and future books.

May you learn the love lessons that are presented to you, and may you have an abundance of authentic love in your life.

I wish you love,

Chérie Carter-Scott, Ph.D.